Get Bendy

Get Bendy

An adventure guide to resilience and discovering your best life

· · · · · · · · · · ·

Michelle Hargrave

ADVANCED PRAISE

"Get Bendy" is a heartfelt and inspiring journey of resilience, brimming with stories that beautifully capture the transformative power of travel and self-discovery.

Through her engaging storytelling, Michelle provides both practical guidance and emotional insights that encourage readers to embrace life's unpredictability with flexibility and joy.

Her candid reflections highlight the profound role of community and self-empowerment in transforming life's challenges into meaningful growth.

Each chapter includes thoughtful exercises that guide readers in applying these insights to their own lives, making the journey toward resilience and personal discovery both accessible and impactful.

This book is a must-read for anyone yearning for adventure, introspection, and a life well-lived.

Carmen Marshall
Founder, Soul Craft, Create A Life You Love Retreats
+ Soul Series Dance
www.CarmenMarshall.com

A beautiful and soul-fuelled reminder that life is meant to be experienced in all its dimensions. This magnificent read is a loving and powerful reminder to live life to the fullest, seek adventure and experience joy! Where story-telling meets life- transforming! Thank you, Michelle, for this beautiful gift.

-Lee Marie Jacobs, author of *Beautiful Money*

Published by Bentley Press

ISBN: 978-1-0691633-0-1
ISBN: 978-1-0691633-1-8 (eBook)

Cover design by Tanya von Ness
Author photo by 2 the 9's Photography

DEDICATION

To Jana, who makes every adventure better.
And Kris, who takes the adventure to another level.
Time spent with you both is my favourite thing.

CONTENTS

ACKNOWLEDGMENTS

I am forever grateful that my path crossed with Alicia Dunams. Without her, you would not be holding this book! From helping me discover the theme of my vision, to encouraging me to serve in even bigger ways, to guiding me through the entire book writing and publishing process, thank you. I simply cannot thank you enough.

To Peg Moline, brilliant editor, who understood what I was trying to say and made it even better.

To Chantal Diaz, who saw something in me when no one else did. Your wisdom and perseverance and sometimes tough love helped me not only become debt-free, but also abundant. Thank you.

To my Remote Year family, thank you for sharing the experience and giving me so many stories to remember. You are all a part of my journey and I love you.

Tamara McLean, my dear friend who shouted "heck ya" when I first shared my book idea. Your friendship means the world to me.

Teresa Ciolfitto, my sounding board and asker of great questions. Thank you for celebrating each small win with me.

ACKNOWLEDGMENTS

Colleen Bognar, who always approved my time off requests so I could write. Thank you for your never-ending support and encouragement.

Ashley Hyndman, my amazing sister-in-law and believer in big dreams. Thank you for your insights, your feedback and your love.

To my brother Kris, who introduced me to travel and continues to inspire me with his own adventures. Your unique perspective and fierce love for your family astounds me.

To my sister, Jana. Every travel journal I have mentions how much I miss you or how much better I felt after talking to you. You are my best friend. I'd be lost without you.

To my parents. You may not have always understood the path I chose but you let me pursue it and cheered me on every step. Thank you.

To all my lovely family, friends and colleagues who encouraged me to tell my stories, thank you. I hope you enjoy.

INTRODUCTION

For a long time, I've wanted to write a book. I started and stopped several times and struggled to find a topic that would hold my interest to the end.

It took me getting really sick and questioning where I was on my journey, what had I accomplished, and what I still wanted to achieve, to realize writing a book was at the top of my list of things still to do.

And when I started to look deeper into what I wanted to write about and the stories that I wanted to share, there was a common theme of resilience.

When I started my travel blog in 2017, people told me how much they enjoyed reading my stories. After I returned from my year around the world, I was surprised by how many people reached out to say they missed my writing.

At that time, I had started to retreat from the world, embarrassed by my financial situation and unsure how to turn things around. I stopped writing because it was too hard to share what I was going through; it was too raw and I wasn't ready to be that vulnerable. I eventually asked for help but I still didn't want to publicly share what felt like failure. I simply wanted to hide until I could be "presentable" to the world again.

I've realized now that life is full of ups and downs and true friends love you through it all. I didn't need to be perfect for my friends or family to love me. But sometimes it can be hard to see that, when you're in the middle of darkness, when you're lower than you've ever been, when you can't see the way out.

I've always been independent and proud of the things I've accomplished on my own, but looking back, I can see where asking for help would have made the journey easier, and maybe even more fun. This is a book about choices, the good and the bad, and learning to "get bendy" as we flow through life.

Life is full of uncertainty and you're going to be thrown a few curveballs. How do you bounce back from those unexpected experiences? Is there a secret to working through the process and coming out on the other side? Let me share my stories and see if you can learn from my mistakes.

Get Bendy is fun, it's playful, and it represents my outlook on life.

Travel is such a brilliant place to practice resilience because travel never goes smoothly. It never goes as planned. Something is absolutely going to go sideways. When I first started traveling, I didn't realize that. I had my plans and my itineraries and my schedule, and the world laughed.

I'm sure this has happened to everyone at some point, but my luggage got lost. (Okay, they don't say "lost" it was simply "delayed.") I was flying to Split, Croatia to start my one-year travel adventure and I had packed meticulously. I was going to be travelling to 12 countries in 12 months, so I had to really think about what I was packing—cold weather, warm weather, comforts from home, practical items. It took me weeks to figure out what to pack in this one suitcase, one suitcase I was going to have for a whole year, and keep it under 50 pounds.

My sister dropped me off at the airport in Kelowna, B.C., we said a tearful "goodbye" and I was on my way through Vancouver, then Frankfurt and finally Split.

If you've ever flown through Frankfurt, you know it's a massive airport. We arrived behind schedule and the gate agent said, "You're probably not going to make your flight. If you hustle, you might be able to make it."

If you know me, you know I don't hustle. I'm not a runner. I'm not athletic. I'm more of a slow stroller, a take-in-life-along-the-way kind of girl.

But I wanted to make my connection so I moved as fast as I could. Down this hallway, around the corner, down another hallway, through security again, around a corner, another hallway, it was never-ending. Frankfurt Airport is never-ending, and I vowed to never book a flight connecting through that airport again.

I finally arrived at my gate, and there was nobody around, not a single person. All of that hustling and I'm sweating and I'm hungry and I'm thirsty, and I missed the plane anyway. My heart sunk.

But then this guy pops out from behind a pillar and says, "Are you my Canadian girl?" "Ummm, yes?" I said. "Great, we're waiting for you." They had held the plane for me!

I got onto the plane, found my seat and got settled in for the last leg of my journey.

We landed in Split, Croatia, and all the luggage was coming off. One by one people grabbed their suitcase and headed towards customs. Eventually the conveyor belt stopped, and my suitcase was not there. I had hustled to make the connection, but my suitcase did not make the plane in Frankfurt. My precious suitcase with everything I thought I needed for the next year was missing.

I'm about to meet the group of 50 people who I will spend the next year with. Strangers from around the world — and you only get one chance to make a first impression. Everyone has their suitcases and they're getting on the bus, but they realize I'm standing there with nothing. "Where's your suitcase?" someone said. "I don't know, it's not here," I responded.

In that moment, I had a choice. I could have a tantrum and yell at the airline staff (something I would never do!), I could have a big cry and fall apart, or I could just go with the flow and trust that my suitcase would eventually show up.

I decided to go with the flow. I found a lovely staff person, gave them the address of where I was going to be staying, hopped on the bus, and away we went.

That night we were having a "meet and greet" at a waterfront restaurant. I was still wearing the same clothes I had travelled all day in. I didn't have a toothbrush. I didn't have deodorant. I hadn't packed anything like that in my carry on because it never occurred to me that my suitcase wouldn't arrive when I did.

Again, I had a choice. I could have stayed in my apartment and felt sorry for myself, or I could splash some water on my face, go out and meet my new friends. The choice was easy — of course I'd go out and meet everyone. As I was standing in this crowd of people, I realized this is what it's all about. This is why we travel — to have adventures, to meet new people, to try new things. It doesn't matter what you're wearing or if your hair is a little wild (they would come to learn my hair is almost always wild no matter what I do).

An interesting thing happened. We were trying to remember everybody's names and where they come from and what they do. I quickly became known as the girl who didn't have her luggage. Several people came up to me later and said, "I can't believe how calm you were. I can't believe how much fun you were having. If that had been me, this whole trip would have been ruined. I would have been in my room crying. I wouldn't have come out."

I really liked how that felt. Yes, I was calm, and I did have fun. I made that choice. I chose to embrace the belief that my suitcase was going to show up. I chose how I wanted to accept that moment. I believed everything would be fine and I could figure it out.

I'd love to say I learned my lesson and always pack a spare change of clothes in my carry on, but not always. Sometimes I risk it and sometimes it doesn't work out. But either way, I choose to embrace the adventure.

That's what I mean by "get bendy" — to just go with the flow and trust that everything is going to work out exactly how it's meant to.

Looking back at my travels and life choices, I can see the steps that helped me move through things and I can see where I went wrong, and I think it could help people. That's why I wrote this book.

I hope my stories make you laugh or see the world from a new perspective. I hope you find a nugget or two to help guide your own choices. And most of all, I hope you realize that you are amazing and everything you need to live your best life is already inside of you!

Birthday thoughts at Kliss Fortress, Croatia

City walls of Dubrovnik, Croatia

Plitvice National Park, Croatia

Exploring Old Town Split, Croatia

Arrived in Split, Croatia (minus my luggage)

Chapter 1

GET BENDY

"Stay committed to your decisions but stay flexible in your approach."

Tony Robbins

Getting bendy is about being adaptable, because life requires you to be flexible. We can't be rigid in our thinking and our behaviors and expect to find joy in life. Getting bendy is about recognizing the situation, accepting it and choosing how to respond.

In February 2014, I was having sushi with my friend Tammy as part of our monthly lunch dates. I told her about this retreat in Bali called "Create a Life You Love" by Carmen Marshall. Carmen is someone I had admired from a distance for years. We were both part of a nutritional company and I had seen her speak several times. She was smart and kind and living the type of lifestyle I wanted for myself. I remembered the saying of "You are the product of the five people you surround yourself with," and so I wanted to spend time with Carmen and learn everything she had to teach. But the retreat was more than I had in my savings account and a trip to Bali wasn't something I had planned on doing that year.

Tammy listened to me excitedly talk about this retreat and simply said, "You have to go." And I jumped in with my excuses: "It's too expensive, it's too far away, I don't know if I can get the time off."

And she said, "If you don't go, you're crazy. Go!" "Okay, okay," I replied, "I'm booking it right now."

So I went back to the office, requested the time off and opened the website to book my spot in the retreat. There were only 12 spots available, and I hoped I hadn't waited too long.

Success! I was in!

The retreat was in May, so I had three months to get ready. I booked my flights and started the homework to prepare. One of the assignments was to read *The Passion Test — The Effortless Path to Discovering Your Life Purpose*, by Janet Bray Attwood and Chris Attwood. (I highly recommend checking this out if you're looking to create a life you love.)

May arrived before I knew it and I was off on my grand adventure. My friend Diane drove me to the Kelowna airport for a 7:45pm flight to Vancouver. My next flight left at 2am so I had almost five hours to wait. My older brother, Orrin, met me for tea before I went through security so that helped spend the time. I boarded the 2am flight heading to Taipei, the capital of Taiwan and a 13-hour flight. The flight was full but I had a window seat so I could see what was happening outside and also lean against the window to try to sleep. I arrived in Taipei and had a three-hour layover — enough time to stretch my legs, explore the airport and eat the snacks I had packed. The next flight to Denpasar (Bali) was six hours but I had the whole row to myself and was able to get some proper sleep.

I finally arrived and was welcomed with 31-degree (Celsius) heat — so hot and humid! I zipped through customs and went outside to find the driver my boyfriend had booked for me (after a taxi incident in Buenos Aires, he insisted on booking drivers for me, more about that in Chapter 4). There must have been more than 200 drivers waiting for passengers, but I saw a sign with my name on it, and introduced myself to Agune, my driver. He didn't speak much English, but he knew where my hotel was, and off we went.

It was very hectic, with lots of traffic and people and noise. They drive on the left-hand side of the road, which always takes some getting used to and contributes to a feeling of chaos. Between the jet lag and the traffic, I was overwhelmed with my introduction to Bali.

As Agune pulled up in front of the hotel, he stopped at a gate and two security guards came out. They started looking under the car with long sticks that had mirrors on the end. I asked Agune what they were looking for. "Bombs," was all he said, as if this was something normal. "Umm, bombs?" I replied. This was not normal for me.

I checked into the hotel, thinking, "Okay, we're worried about bombs here, that's interesting." I later learned there had been bombings in Bali in 2002 that killed more than 200 people, so security measures had rightfully changed.

The hotel room was beautiful. It was all marble and all white. White furniture, white floors, white artwork, white linens. It had floor to ceiling windows looking out over a pool. It was everything I imagined Bali would be. I was exhausted and excited to experience Bali. I opened my suitcase to start unpacking and in the top right-hand corner, there was an empty space. "That's weird," I thought. What was there? I remember my suitcase was full so there shouldn't be any empty spaces. Then I realized, that's where my camera was. I had it packed in my checked bag and now it was gone.

I thought, "Oh, it must be here somewhere, maybe it slipped down." So I'm digging through my suitcase, looking, looking, looking, and of course, it's not there. It's gone.

This was an expensive camera, and it had photos from other trips on the memory disc. I had so many plans for the next two weeks in Bali and now I didn't have a camera to capture it. I was crushed. I felt violated — someone had opened up my suitcase, gone through my things and stolen something. That didn't feel good.

I laid down on the bed and had a big cry. "This whole trip is ruined," I sobbed.

A Lesson, Not a Loss

But as I was laying there, I remembered an article I had read on the plane about letting go of who you think you should be and living an authentic life. I remembered agreeing and thinking about what I needed to let go of. I didn't think letting go meant losing my camera, but it was a good place to start!

I had a thought; "What is the gift in this?" How could I reframe it from *I'm a victim, somebody stole from me* to *this thing happened and now I can do this.* And it came to me — now I get to be present for every experience I'm having. I don't have to worry about capturing the event and taking multiple angles and worrying about the lighting, all of those things we like to do when we're traveling to want to get the right photo. I could simply be in the moment. I could experience the sights and sounds and just have that memory for myself. And I was grateful my camera was stolen at the beginning of the trip and not after, when it would have been full of photos.

As soon as I reframed it, I felt so much lighter. I felt peace and said to myself, "Okay, let's start this adventure. Let's see how this is going to be without that camera. It's just a thing. Let's go explore."

And that really got me thinking about when you travel, you need to be adaptable, be flexible, and *get bendy*. It's really about taking a look at the situation, being mindful and staying calm, and realizing that you can figure it out.

Agune picked me up the next day to drive to Ubud and Soul-Shine, a wellness centre owned by Michael Franti and where I'd be spending the next week in Carmen Marshall's retreat. Along the way, I saw familiar brands from back home — Starbucks, McDonalds, Century 21 — all mixed in with tailors and scooter rentals and souvenir shops.

We arrived at a dirt road and Agune said this was the place. I was skeptical but got out and started walking down the path. Along the way, beautiful words had been painted on stones.

"Relax."

I took a few more steps.

"Breathe."

I continued.

"Let your soul shine."

Step.

"Imagine."

Step, step.

"Follow your heart."

By the time I reached the front desk, I felt calm and peaceful. I was exactly where I needed to be and ready to dive into personal development, make new friends and have new experiences.

As I got settled in and met the other retreat participants, I told them my camera had been stolen. They were so kind and simply said, "No worries, we'll just share our photos with you."

Our group of 12 people exchanged email addresses and decided to share all of their photos. And what a beautiful idea, because it allowed other people to be more present. For those who wanted to take pictures, they could. For those of us who couldn't or didn't want to, we could still access the photos. We were going to be at this retreat together for the week and we had started off becoming friends, looking for ways to help each other, to support each other, to make the week memorable.

Having my camera stolen created an opportunity. It created community. It created a great idea. There was a co-creation that happened in that moment to come together and solve a problem. And it resulted in a beautiful collection of photos because everyone has a different perspective in life, and everyone has a different camera angle. It also meant I could be in some of the photos. What a gift!

The "Create a Life You Love" retreat was a pivotal moment for me in learning to clarify my own passions and define how I wanted my life to look and feel. After going through Carmen's process, I knew I could create a different way of living, and had the belief, confidence and tools to pursue my dreams.

Traveling makes me feel alive. It opens your mind to new ways of thinking and new ways of living. It changes your perspective; it helps you get clear about what's really important in your life. Whether you travel alone or with friends, you learn things about yourself that might surprise you.

I've learned I value my sleep and get cranky if someone wakes me up before I'm ready. I've learned to always pack snacks because I can't think straight if I'm hungry. I've learned I can't go all day from one activity to the next — I need rest breaks and naps throughout the day. And I've learned that doing something new often requires great concentration and sometimes help from a friend.

Create a Life You Love Retreat, Bali (Michelle at far right, front)

Desa Seni Eco Resort, Bali

SoulShine Retreat, Bali

Turning off the Autopilot

In 2006, my youngest brother, Kris, decided to travel to Australia and New Zealand for a year. And my sister, Jana, decided to join him for six months. Feeling a big sense of missing out, I asked my boss if I could take all my vacation days at once and go too. She agreed and I flew out to join them for six weeks.

Coming from Canada, we drive on the right-hand side of the road, and as you probably know, in Australia, they drive on the left-hand side. As I was the only one older than 25, I was the only one allowed to drive the rental car. *How hard could it be?* I thought (this was before my trips to countries like Bali where they also drive on the left-hand side).

It's actually really hard, because your brain has been wired one way for so long and now you're asking it to do the opposite of what it knows. For starters, I've always gotten into the vehicle on the left side, and now that was the passenger seat. The windshield wipers are always to the right of the steering wheel and now that's where the turn signal is. Everything was flipped around, and my brain was in overdrive — talk about getting bendy!

It was more challenging than I thought, so I ended up announcing what I was going to do — before doing it — and my sister confirmed my thinking. As I came up to a roundabout, I'd say, "I'm going to be going this way, and I'm going to use my right signal here." And she'd say, "Yep, that's right," or "No, you can't turn here." I lost track of how many times she said "No, no!" We worked together as a team to navigate our way through Australia.

I was fine on the open highway when you're going straight and there are no towns. But as soon as we came to a big city, and there were multi-lane roundabouts and multi-lane toll bridges, I realized I had to really use a different part of my brain and think about what I was doing.

After years of driving, many of us don't think about it at all. You hop in the car and drive to work or the grocery store or a friend's house. Sometimes you don't even remember the route you took and are surprised when you've arrived.

But when you take yourself to another country where the rules are different, you quickly realize how much you rely on routine. For lots of people, they're not just driving on automatic, they're living their lives on automatic. Never stopping to think about what they're really doing, and if they're going where they want to go.

It's easy to do the same thing over and over. You get up, you eat the same breakfast, you drive the same way to work. And one day you wake up and all of the sudden you're 40 or you're 50 or 60 and you're wondering, "What happened? How did I get here?"

Our brain likes routine, it likes us to do the same, predictable behaviour — that's safe. New and unknown is risky, and our brain's job is to keep us safe. But to fully experience life, we need to shake things up and keep our brain guessing what's going to happen next!

The experience of driving through Australia woke me up. I was aware of each decision I made. I didn't take action without checking in. All of my senses were on high alert because everything was new, and nothing was known.

When I returned to Canada, I wanted to keep that feeling of experiencing each day to the fullest, of knowing I'm alive, of not letting my brain slip into routine and let life pass me by. So I asked myself, "What can I do in my day-to-day life to bring some of those feelings along?"

I researched some ideas, including using your non-dominant hand to brush your teeth, taking the stairs if you normally use the elevator, or choosing a different stall in the bathroom at work.

I started simple. I changed my route to work every day and drove a different way. My brain was quick to respond with thoughts like: *Whoa, what are we doing? Where are we going? I don't know this road. This isn't the fastest road to work. What are we doing here?*

I smiled as I drove down tree-lined streets, their branches creating a magical arch above. I watched a farmer cutting hay in his field. I laughed watching kids skip along to school. All of my senses were firing. My eyes were seeing things I'd never seen before. I was hearing new sounds, smelling new scents and feeling alive.

I realized there is a whole world of things happening while I'm simply driving to work, and I had never noticed before because I took the same route.

As the week went on, I thought, *What else can I do?* I started choosing a different place for lunch every day. One day I went to a park I had never been to before, the next day I went to a restaurant I'd only driven by and never tried, another day I called a friend to meet me for lunch. I tried to do something different every day for lunch and see what happened.

I felt...new. I felt different. I felt alive. My brain didn't know what to expect. *Is she going to go left? Is she going to go right? Is she going to go up the stairs? Is she going to take the elevator? We don't know. We don't know what's happening!* And that's how you know you're alive. The feeling of aliveness comes from newness, variety, changing things up, living life not on automatic but living life in an agile, adaptable, flexible way.

Because nothing happens the way it's planned when you travel, travel is a great way to feel alive and practice your resilience skills.

Byron Bay, Australia

Fraser Island, Australia

Jana and I with our rental car in Australia

Flying Solo: Go With the Flow

In 2008, I decided to do a trip by myself to Vietnam, Cambodia and Thailand. Originally Kris and I were going to do a Europe trip, but we had to postpone so I booked a last-minute trip to Asia without doing any research. The flight was 12.5 hours from Vancouver to Hong Kong, a two-hour layover, then a one-hour flight to Hanoi, Vietnam.

From the moment I arrived, everything was uncertain. I stood outside the airport surrounded by people and animals and vehicles and noise and incredible heat. Scooters and bikes zipped by. Traffic was crazy with no sense of direction or rules and constant honking. There was even a man on a bicycle leading a water buffalo down the highway!

I wondered what I was doing and who I thought I was to set out on this adventure alone. I often get these grand ideas and set off full of confidence, only to feel uncertain and question every decision I made leading up to the moment. But I had made the choice to have an adventure and had to believe it would lead to something good. You never know where a decision will take you, but you take a step forward and trust yourself.

However, that first step felt impossible. I stood on the street with no sidewalks, no lights, no crosswalks, no sense of order and a steady stream of cars, trucks, motorbikes, bicycles and even animals. As I stood there pondering, an older lady came up, grabbed my arm and started crossing the street. "Don't stop," she said, and before I knew it, we were safely on the other side! The key to crossing streets in Vietnam was to simply step out with purpose and keep moving. (Great life lesson, too!)

We don't have many passenger trains in Canada, and I had this romantic idea about taking an overnight train. Trains are popular in Asia, so it seemed like a great plan, and I booked a ticket from Hanoi to Hue (about 700 kms and 12 hours).

I should have known things were going to go sideways because that's what happens with travel, and when you choose an adventure. It started off with trying to get on board.

People in Asia are smaller than Canadians. They're typically quite short and petite, so other things also tend to be smaller. As I went to step up into the train, my backpack got stuck — my backpack was too wide for the doorframe. I was literally stuck — I couldn't move forward and I couldn't step back. I started laughing, and the more I laughed, the more I realized I had no strength. I could hear people behind me speaking in other languages and assumed they were saying something like, "Get this Canadian girl on the train."

But I couldn't. I was just standing there in the stairwell thinking, *Okay, I'm too big for the train. What now*? Eventually, with the help of other people shoving me, I got through the doorframe and onto the train. "I'm here, okay, this is still going to be an amazing, romantic life experience," I told myself.

I'm looking at my ticket, where I'm going, and walking down the hallway. I'm touching both sides of the hallway, by the way. And I'm not a large person by Canadian standards. I'm 5.8" and average weight. But in Asia, I felt like a giant.

I found my cabin and there were no seats but there were people in there. And not only people, but there were also people with chickens in there. They brought their chickens on the train and I'm thinking, *I've never seen that before. Okay, okay, traveling with chickens isn't a problem.*

Then I looked around the small room for a place to sit. And all I see is a wall of bunk beds, three on one side and three on the other. And I'm thinking, *How am I going to climb up to this top one? It's a long way up there.* There are chickens and there are people and nobody's speaking English and I'm a giant and feeling flushed. I guess I looked a little confused or a little distressed perhaps, because someone indicated they would take the top bunk. *Phew.*

They climbed up to the top and I sat down on the lower one. I started to feel a bit calmer and gave myself a pep talk. "Okay, I'm on this train in Vietnam, I'm doing the thing. I'm here with people and chickens and what an amazing experience. You've got this."

I decided to get settled in and ready for bed. I pulled out my night cream and my toothpaste and toothbrush and all of the things that I would normally need to get ready for bed. Off I went to find the washroom.

I strolled back down the hallway looking for the washroom. I found it, opened the door, and froze. There was a hole in the floor and I could see the train tracks rushing by. I backed up to confirm this was in fact the washroom. Yup. This was the bathroom — a hole in the floor and a small sink. There wasn't a mirror or soap or a hand towel or even a paper towel. I decided I could skip a night of brushing my teeth and washing my face. Those were things I would normally do, and I took it for granted that people around the world would have similar nighttime routines.

By the way: I would recommend throwing the word "normal" out the window because nothing is normal when you're traveling. If you expect things to be how they are back home, you are going to be very disappointed. And isn't that the whole point of traveling — to open your mind to new ideas of ways of living, to have new experiences?

Some experiences are amazing, and you want to implement them when you get back home. Some of them are not amazing and you can be really grateful for what you have when you do get back home. But every trip is an adventure and you learn something new about yourself and the world. You have a new experience.

And so that was the moment I let go of my idea of romantic train travel and learned to have no expectations, to simply get bendy and go with the flow.

Hanoi, Vietnam

Hoi An, Vietnam

Whale Island, Vietnam

Ho Chi Minh Museum, Vietnam

With just about every experience I have while travelling, I learn something important. So, in every chapter I'll share what I've learned, and give you some questions to prompt your own consideration, as well as a little exercise.

The Get Bendy lesson here is to ask yourself: "Where's the gift in this experience?"

Get Bendy Reflection Questions

- What can I control in this situation?
- What can I accept about this experience?

Get Bendy Exercise

Close your eyes and visualize a recent frustrating situation, like a delayed flight. Mentally separate the elements into two categories: What you can control (your reactions, choices) and what you can't control (external factors, like weather).

Focus on how shifting your attention to what you can control helps you feel more empowered and calm. Imagine handling a similar situation positively in the future, emphasizing your ability to choose your response.

Chapter 2

ALL ABOUT YOU

"Love yourself first and everything else falls into line."

Lucille Ball

Self-awareness is the next skill in developing resilience. It's about recognizing and acknowledging your emotions because you need to understand your thoughts, emotions, and behaviours, and how they affect both you and those around you.

Knowing yourself helps you figure out what triggers you and what you need to be able to bounce back. And it's going to be different for everyone. What works for me might not work for you.

Knowing what you need and making sure you give that to yourself in every situation, whether you're traveling, whether you're at home, whether you're with your family. You still need to be aware of things that might trigger you, how you might react to that, and what you can do to help yourself gracefully move through it.

Self-awareness means constantly questioning and doing self-reflection on what are your thoughts, what are your feelings, and what are your physical sensations in this particular moment.

Learning to Listen to Myself

Back to my solo trip to Asia in 2008, I finished the train ride through Vietnam and was getting ready to head to Cambodia. Vietnam was beautiful and the people were friendly, generous and kind. And the food was delicious. I discovered deep fried bananas with chocolate and ice cream. I think I ate it every day!

As much as I enjoyed Vietnam, I was ready to move to the next country and explore Cambodia. I had two options — ride in a van or fly. The guide said the drive would take about eight hours on a dusty, bumpy road. And the flight was less than an hour.

I took a moment and asked myself, "What do I need?" It was a moment of checking in. A van ride would give me the chance to see the countryside and maybe some cool things, but it would be a bumpy ride, long and dusty. That might be uncomfortable and not so fun. Flying would be short, and I'd get there fast.

I decided I wanted to fly, so I booked the flight with a couple people I'd met along the way. Others chose the van, and we all planned to meet up later in Cambodia, but I didn't see them for hours. When they finally arrived, those who took the van ride were wrecked. People were holding their backs in pain. Not only was it a bumpy road, but the van only had wooden benches for seats. I definitely made the right decision, and I was so thankful I had listened to myself and asked what I needed.

Gob Smacked by the Wealth Gap

Since I had flown, I was rested and ready to go so, we went to explore and walk around Phnom Penh. As we walked along, I was shocked by the striking contrasts. There were people lying in the street, not just homeless but destitute. And there were children and disabled people, sick and starving.

There was garbage everywhere and people were lying in filth. And then there were Range Rovers and Hummers driving by, mansions behind large gates, and the Royal Palace full of gold, silver and diamonds. The gap between poor and rich was so wide, I couldn't comprehend it.

The people in my group simply stepped over and around the homeless and sick, marveling at the fact beer was only $1 and planning how drunk they could get for $20.

Meanwhile, I'm thinking how $20 would change lives. $20 would feed a family. $20 would make you rich in this country. I started to feel guilty. These people had nothing. We were just walking down their sidewalk looking for a place to eat and they were literally starving to death on their own streets. My heart was heavy.

The next day I signed up for a tour that included the Killing Fields and S21 — a genocide concentration camp. During the tour,

I learned about the genocide that killed at least 2 million people between 1975 and 1979, nearly 25 per cent of Cambodia's population in 1975.

"The Cambodian genocide was the systematic persecution and killing of Cambodian citizens by the Khmer Rouge under the leadership of Prime Minister of Democratic Kampuchea, Pol Pot," according to Wikipedia.

"The Khmer Rouge regime arrested and executed anyone whom it suspected of having connections with the former Cambodian government along with anyone whom it suspected of having connections with foreign governments, as well as professionals, intellectuals, the Buddhist monkhood, and ethnic minorities," the site continued. "Even those people who were stereotypically thought of as having intellectual qualities, such as wearing glasses or speaking multiple languages, were executed out of fear that they would rebel against the Khmer Rouge."

There were horrible crimes I could not begin to understand.

My fellow travelers had done their research and knew Cambodia's history but not me. I had done no research, and learning about these crimes that took place in my lifetime shook me to my core.

I was a blissfully ignorant little girl playing with my dolls in Canada, while in another part of the world, people were being killed. They were wiping out a whole generation of people. And it shocked me. It was one of the first times I came face-to-face with the dark side of humanity and realized there's so much more going on in the world than my little experience. Seeing the cells where people were crammed in, with ceilings so low you couldn't fully stand up, and mass graves where someone's loved ones lay, are images that still haunt my dreams.

The next day, we left for Siem Reap, an eight-hour journey by bus through the Cambodian countryside. It was a good opportunity to see the beauty of this country and decompress from the images I had seen the day before.

I woke early the following day to catch the 4am bus to watch the sunrise at Angkor Wat. It was a mystical and magical morning as the sun slowly rose above the ancient ruins. There's something peaceful and wonderful about seeing a sunrise when you travel, to see the world waking up to start a new day. I spent the day exploring the temples and walking through history. There was a lightness and curiosity to my steps as I spent time in nature and wondered who had walked these paths before me. I felt the heaviness of the past few days lift. There is darkness in the world but there is also so much light.

To wrap up the trip, I flew to Bangkok and planned to spend a few days before heading north to Chaing Mai. The pollution in Bangkok was worse than I'd ever experienced, and traffic was constant gridlock.

We headed out to explore the surrounding streets, but I didn't last long. The poverty, the children, the sex trade and all sorts of things I had never seen before — broke my heart. Absolutely broke my heart. And I was traveling alone so I had nobody to talk to about it. Nobody to go back to the hotel at the end of the day and decompress with and be like, "Whoa, this is heavy. This was hard. This was not what I was expecting."

I sat in my hotel room alone and I cried and cried and cried. I thought, *How do people live with this? How is this okay? How are we just letting these things happen?* And I decided I couldn't go on. I was exhausted. I was emotionally drained. I was unprepared to see the things that I saw. But I still had another two weeks before I was supposed to fly home.

This trip was impacting my mental health. I felt a deep, deep sadness, and guilt for having so much. I didn't know how to help. I didn't know what I could do. I was too sad to move but knew I had to talk to someone.

I dusted myself off, left the hotel and went in search of a payphone (I didn't have a cellphone in 2008). I needed to talk to someone who would listen and give me some unbiased advice. Was I overreacting? Was there a lesson I needed to learn here and just needed to stick it out? I didn't know anymore.

I found a payphone on a street corner a few blocks away and I called my big brother, Orrin, collect. He listened, between my sobs, as I explained all the feelings that were overwhelming me. And he said, "Come home, come home." I said, "I can't. I've got two more weeks. I've got a plane ticket." And he said, "You don't have to stay. If this is too hard, if this is too much, come home."

And just hearing that, I thought, "*Yeah, you know, I can go home. I'm going to give myself permission to come home early and change my flight and come home, because that's part of being flexible and adaptable and knowing your needs.*" I knew I was in crisis. I was in trouble. And I didn't know what to do. And I had no support there with me. I had no one to talk to. I had no one who understood. I felt hopeless at the time.

Being able to identify the emotions I was feeling, to be aware of what was going on around me, and being reminded to take care of myself, saved me.

I went home.

But when I got there, my house felt huge. I felt like four families could live in it and here I was, just one person, having all this. I felt guilt and anger and shame. I felt I didn't deserve to have so much when people in the world had so little.

I had no patience for the people around me who whined about a parking ticket, or complained about their job, or how long it took to drive to work. "Well, at least you have a car," I snapped. "At least you have a job. At least you have all these things you take for granted. Don't you know there are people in Cambodia and Thailand who don't have anything to eat? They're starving on the streets. And you're going to complain that it took you an hour to drive in your fancy car to your air-conditioned office?"

I was angry.

I had never experienced this type of anger, and I didn't know how to process it. Recognizing I needed help, I sought out counselling. It was the best decision I made to take care of myself. My counsellor explained reverse culture shock and helped me understand the intense feelings I was having.

I was frustrated, alienated and critical of my own culture. Things that were previously normal to me now stood out. And I felt like no one really wanted to hear about my experience because they couldn't relate to it.

I felt like I had to be reintroduced into Canadian society and to the Canadian style of living. And it felt so wasteful and unfair. Traveling opens your eyes and causes you to expand, and like an elastic that's been stretched, you can never go back to who you were before once you've seen and experienced something like that.

The small little world I had in Canada was expanded, and it was a hard adjustment. But in terms of my own self-awareness, I was able to tune into myself in Cambodia, recognize I was emotionally exhausted, and give myself permission to put my mental health at rest. But I also saw myself in the bigger picture of the world, having a social awareness of the problems, the uncertainty, the abject poverty in the world, and that I'm privileged and blessed.

My counsellor gave me tools to help work through the reverse culture shock, including finding something that brought me joy every day. Small, simple things like a fluffy white cloud or the fresh smell after a rainfall. When I struggled, he asked me to think about the things I had done as a child and if I could remember what I loved doing when I was little. I instantly thought of peddling my bicycle down the road, a big smile on my face, the wind blowing in my hair and feeling unstoppable.

As an adult, I didn't own a bike and had forgotten how it brought me joy. An avid cyclist, my counsellor offered to meet me at the local bike shop and help me pick out a bike. With my new bike, helmet and water bottle, I rode every week, discovering new trails and finding peace being in nature. Day by day, week by week, month by month, I slowly started to adapt and find ways to integrate my travel experience into my life.

Once I started feeling more balanced, I wanted to find ways I could help, specifically people in the countries to which I had traveled. I felt like I had a connection to them and was in a position to do something.

A Way to Help From Home

A friend of mine introduced me to an organization called Kiva. Kiva is an international non-profit with a mission to expand financial access to underserved communities (www.kiva.org/about). They do this through crowdfunding loans. For as little as $25, you can set up your first loan and start making a difference. You can filter by the country where you'd like to lend money to, by industry, or gender or groups. You can help people whose loans are almost fully funded or those who haven't received any funds yet.

I decided I wanted to focus on women in Cambodia, Vietnam and Thailand who were in agriculture. These women were looking for funding to buy more fertilizer for their fields, or to buy a cow so they could sell the milk in the market, or to buy a pig they could breed and sell the piglets.

The requests were simple, but I was in awe of these women living in a challenging country and rising above to find ways to make a living and care for their families. They were looking for a $100 loan or $50 loan to start their business. Yes, it's a loan and they repay you — it's not even a donation. And I remembered all the women who have supported me and encouraged me in my career, and now it was my turn to give back.

Not only is there joy in helping someone, but there's also joy seeing them succeed. You can read about the borrower's story and how they're doing. You can share their story and encourage others to lend. It's a small way to help the women in those countries be empowered to build their business and change their way of life. And you might not be aware of that unless you traveled there.

Asia was an extreme experience for me and it changed me. But it didn't stop me from travelling or continuing to seek new experiences.

Angkor Thom, Siem Reap, Cambodia

Homestay at French Colonial home off Mekong River

Floating down the Mekong River

Seeking Peace in Prague: The Yoga Class From Hell

During a year of traveling around the world, I was living in Prague for a month. There was a yoga studio around the corner from my apartment, so I walked over and signed up for a 30-day unlimited pass. With all the walking I'd been doing while traveling, taking some time to stretch seemed like a good idea.

My first class went well, although I didn't realize it was hot yoga. The instructor was from California so I had no trouble understanding her, but she encouraged me to try any class, regardless of whether the instructor spoke English.

The next night I decided to try the 7:30pm class, thinking it would be a lovely restorative class before bed. I arrived five minutes early, unrolled my mat, laid down and closed my eyes while adjusting to the heated room.

At 7:30pm, the lights flipped on, and a woman strode to the front of the room speaking in rapid fire Czech. That should have been a sign that I was in over my head. My body said "Run" but my head said "Stay, it's part of the adventure!"

Reminding myself to be open to new things, I decided to stay and see where things led.

It quickly went downhill.

The instructor spoke some English —"no, no" being her favourite. "No, no" as she grabbed my arms to straighten them, "no, no" as she grabbed my feet to bring them closer together, "no, no" as she tilted my head back further. She moved quickly from one pose to the next, yelling in Czech the whole time.

Where was the soft lighting? Where was the lovely yoga music? Where were the gentle words of listening to your body and showing gratitude? Nowhere to be seen or heard. I'm pretty sure I walked into a Czech boot camp disguised as yoga.

I tried my best to keep up but soon felt nauseous and thought it best to lie down. "No, no," she said, pulling my arms to get me back up. "No, no," I responded and laid down again — I was done. With 10 minutes left in the class, I felt *shavasana* was appropriate and I closed my eyes.

Maybe they do yoga differently in Czech or maybe I went to a class beyond my abilities but I'm still glad I went. I did something a local would do and tried something outside my comfort zone.

Prague, Czech Republic   Opportunity awaits in Prague

Prague, Czech Republic

Side trip to Vienna, Austria

Ways to Find Calm

When we talk about self-care, it can be tempting to just think about monthly massages or getting your nails done. But self-care is more than that.

True self-care gives you the energy and the fortitude to be able to go out to work, and to keep going. Consider: What are the things we can do to calm our nervous system, to regulate the nervous system so we can go out and help ourselves in the world? For me, this starts in the morning, and then it's how I wrap up my day. It's something I learned at Carmen's "Create a Life You Love" retreat in Bali and has continued over the years.

When I wake up in the morning, before I jump out of bed and dive into the day like so many of us do, I take a few minutes to map out the day ahead. I visualize how the day is going to go, who I'm going to meet, where we're going to go, the results of a meeting, and really be thoughtful with my plans. I focus on how I want to feel — confident or joyful or peaceful or fun. And then I start the day.

But what really brings it home for me at the end of the day before I go to bed, is I replay the whole day. And if something didn't quite go how I wanted it to, I rewrite it! The brain doesn't know the truth from something that's not true so if you can visualize how you really wanted it to go, then you can fall asleep in that good feeling place.

The Power of Visualization

Mike Tranter is a neuroscientist at the University of California, San Diego, specializing in the neural circuitry within the brain and studies the effect of visualization. He holds a Ph.D. in neuroscience and is author of the bestselling book *A Million Things to Ask a Neuroscientist: The Brain Made Easy.*

"When you close your eyes and visualize something, you engage the neural circuitry in the same way as if you were really experiencing it," explains Tranter. "For example, visualizing your partner will activate the visual cortex in the brain, similar to if you are seeing them in front of you." Simply the act of visualizing can activate associated memories and emotional context, and even alter your heart rate. "Your brain doesn't really care that you're not actually having the experience, your neurons are still activated."

Visualization works best when what you imagine is as real as possible, so "engage all your senses." When picturing specific scenarios, visualize what you can hear, what you see and even smell, Tranter says. "This will cement those experiences in your brain much better."[1]

And if you really want to take care of yourself, add gratitude to your nightly routine. After I've reimagined how my day went, I put both hands up in the air and look at my fingers. I use my fingers to count down 10 things I'm grateful for that day.

---

1 https://www.forbes.com/sites/jodiecook/2022/01/12/
how-entrepreneurs-can-leverage-visualization-a- neuroscientist-explains/

10. I'm grateful the sun was shining today.

9. I'm so happy I got to meet Alicia and share an amazing dinner.

8. I'm thankful I talked to my sister.

7. I'm grateful for this comfy, king-sized bed.

6. Thank you for my strong legs that helped me walk around downtown.

5. What a gorgeous tree on my street! I love how it provides shade during my walk.

4. Thank you for showing me the cutest dog at the café today.

3. I'm grateful for the kind gentlemen who held the door for me today while I juggled my drink and bags.

2. I'm grateful for my beautiful home that feels like my sanctuary.

1. Thank you for my health.

We practiced this method at the retreat in Bali and it's so simple. Take your time as you go through and count down 10 things. As you fall asleep in a state of gratitude, it changes your sleep, it changes your body. Your body is rested, it can heal, it can do its work at night, and you wake up in the morning, ready for a new day.

I remind myself, by planning the day, visualizing my day, and then being grateful at the end of the day, it brings me peace. It helps me feel calm and ready to take what life throws at me and bounce back from it. I love that. It grounds you.

The Get Bendy lesson here is to give yourself permission to go home. Whether that's literally to go home or spiritually to get grounded. Take a moment. Take three breaths. Give yourself permission.

Get Bendy Reflection Questions

Ask yourself:
- How am I feeling right now? What do I need?
    1. To talk to a friend?
    2. Play some music?
    3. Go outside?
- What can I do to change how I feel right now?
- What does my perfect day look like?

Get Bendy Exercise

Before you fall asleep tonight, try Carmen's "10 fingers of gratitude" exercise. Raise both hands with your fingers extended. Start counting down from 10 and list one thing you're grateful for today. Put one finger down and move to the next one. Keep going until you've listed 10 things you're grateful for, put your hands down and fall asleep in a state of gratitude. See if it changes how you experience the next day.

Chapter 3

FIND JOY

"Attitude is a little thing that makes a big difference."
Winston Churchill

My friend Adrienne once said to me, "Your default emotion is happy!" and for those who know me, I think they'd agree. I'm generally a happy person and believe this attitude has helped me develop my resilience skills.

I believe the world is a good place, that everything is going to work out the way it's supposed to. It's a sense of optimism, that the outcome is going to be successful. And this gives me the strength to keep trying rather than giving up.

But looking deeper, I think happiness is more of a destination, and joy is the journey. Joy is a long-lasting state of being, characterized by contentment and satisfaction with life overall, while happiness is more of a fleeting emotion sparked by a moment of event. So, I seek joy every day, whether I'm travelling or at home.

This quest for joy lead me to a roadblock in 2016, and ultimately a decision that changed my life.

I'd done a bit of traveling here and there, using my vacation time to go on a trip each year. And I was feeling restless. I wanted to travel, but I needed money to travel. And I liked my job as a senior communications specialist for the B.C. government, but the desire to see more of the world was more than an annual vacation could quench.

I thought, *Do I quit my job now, and go travel and see the world while I'm young and healthy, and worry about finances later? Or do I work hard in my career and save up all my money and then go travel later, but risk that I'm not healthy or I'm too old?*

It seemed like it had to be one or the other — career or travel. And I felt frustrated that I had to choose. I told anyone who would listen, "I don't want to choose. I want it all." And they said, "Tough luck. You can't have it all." Silently I told myself, "No, I'm not buying into that way of thinking."

How I COULD Have it All

I continued to think about travel and career and choices and how I could live a life that combined all the things I loved. And, as luck would have it, I stumbled across an ad that said, "Take your job on the road." I clicked the link and landed on a website called Remote Year. It was a new company that was trying to show that great work could be done anywhere. You did not need to be in an office. Take your job and go and work in another country. And I thought, *This is a thing? Tell me more.*

I devoured this website and read about how professionals like me were living and working in cities around the world — they weren't confined to an office or a 9-to-5 schedule. They had found a way to combine a love for travel while still growing their careers or businesses.

It sounded like a dream — a dream I longed to be part of.

I closed the website, thinking, *Wouldn't that be amazing! I'd like to do that but how? My company would never let me.* My mind flooded with doubts.

I thought that was the end of it, but my subconscious wouldn't let go.

My dreams were full of images of me traveling the world, setting up my laptop in cozy coffee shops or on the beach or looking out at stunning views.

My heart ached for this adventure, so two months later I called Remote Year. I wanted it so bad but didn't want to get my hopes up so I started with my best excuse to protect myself from disappointment — "I'd love to do this, but I don't think my employer will go for it."

The admissions advisor kindly encouraged me to apply, advising they had received over 25,000 applications for 75 spots, so simply apply and deal with your employer if you get accepted.

They were accepting 75 people to complete a one-year journey together, travelling to 12 countries, while working and living their lives. You could be a contractor or freelancer, or you could be an employee — it was up to you. They'd provide accommodations, transportation, a co-working office, language lessons and more.

I applied and was invited to the first stage in the process. This was a simple interview with basic "get to know you-" type questions. Who are you? Where are you from? What do you do for work?

Next, I was asked to write an essay about why I wanted to join Remote Year and what I'd bring to the community. They we trying to build a community of 75 people from around the world, so they needed a good mix of personalities and ages and perspectives to make it work.

I made it through that round and into the final stage — an in-depth interview with staff member Josh. He was in Europe so with the time change, it meant my Zoom interview was at 4am.

I was ready. I was up, showered, dressed and looking my best. We chatted for 45 minutes and I felt it had gone well. Josh said they were reviewing all applicants and would be making decisions in the next few weeks. He'd let me know either way.

I tried to carry on with normal life, going to work, getting groceries, seeing friends but inside my heart was racing — was my life about to radically change?

I felt different and wondered if people could see a change in me.

Only a handful of friends knew I had applied; I was afraid to tell too many people in case I wasn't successful.

The sun rises early in the Okanagan during the summer, and I found myself wide awake at 4:30am so I checked my email…

And there it was…

An email telling me they were pleased to invite me to join Remote Year in 2017!

I screamed, I cried, I jumped up and down, my body shook with excitement, tears of joy ran down my face and I kept whispering "thank you thank you thank you."

It was one of those life-defining moments — a moment you know changes you, a moment you will look back on again and again and say, "that was when it all began".

And so, on March 1, 2017, my journey with Remote Year would begin.

I excitedly went to work and told my boss all about this amazing company and that I'd been accepted and what a fantastic opportunity it was. And she said, "Yes, this does sound amazing, but I don't think you'll be able to do your job outside of Canada."

"Ummm…what?"

"What about security? What about technology? What about your personal safety? There are simply too many unknowns," she said.

"No problem," I said. "Let me do some research." I wrote down every objection I could think of and started to talk to people in my company to come up with solutions. I developed a business plan and addressed every possible scenario I could think of that they would want answered. We went back and forth, back and forth, for close to four months before they made a decision.

"Great business plan. Thank you for all your work and research to put this together. But we're just not comfortable with this idea."

It was a "no."

My heart sank. I kept telling myself, "Don't cry, don't cry, don't cry." But it was not all bad news. "You can't do your job outside of Canada, but you can take a leave of absence. This is an amazing opportunity, so go and do it. We'll hold your job for you."

Now I had permission to go, but no money to do it, because I wouldn't be working. So now I had to figure out how I was going to fund this adventure. It was daunting but not impossible because I knew this was the thing I was meant to do — what brought me joy.

I decided the easiest solution was to start my own business. I started a communications company, built a website, got some contracts, and was ready to roll.

What kept me going through the ups and downs was knowing I was pursuing something true for me. Traveling brings me joy and I was willing to figure out any barrier to give myself the opportunity.

I knew this was what I wanted. And I knew it was meant for me. When the company I worked for said no, it would have been easy to just stop right there and say, "The answer's no, it's not possible. I can't do it. It's too hard. I don't know how." All of those thoughts came up for me momentarily, but in my heart I felt, "I am meant to do this. I will find the way." The joy carried me through.

I went and it changed my life. Did it look how I thought it was going to look? Nope. Did I have to get bendy and figure out how to make it work? Heck ya.

Every day, new things came up to figure out. Every week, new challenges arose to solve. I was constantly required to be resilient. Yes, I was meant to be there. Yes, I knew it in my heart. But that didn't mean it was easy. It didn't mean there were no bumps in the road. But when you know, when you're on your path so clearly, it makes it so much easier to bounce back, to be resilient, to find your joy, even on the worst days. Even when I was exhausted and had a really hard day, I reminded myself of the adventure and the big picture. And that kept me going.

Remote Year family (Michelle in the middle of the back row. Photo credit: Chris Hernandez)

Music and Candlelight

I found moments of deep joy throughout that year abroad. My friend Adrienne invited me to join her for a performance of Vivaldi by candlelight at the Baroque Library Hall in Prague. Classical music in a beautiful historical building? Naturally I said, "Yes."

We arrived and found we had front row seats. The usher brought us each a glass of champagne and we looked around the old hall. Not as large as we expected but the ceiling was curved and covered with intricate paintings.

There were four seats on a small stage. The musicians arrived, silently taking their places. The maestro walked in with a round of applause, and they began.

The music that filled the room took my breath away. It literally sent shivers through my body. The sound was powerful, and I wondered at how so few instruments could make such an incredible sound.

On and on they played, each song full of highs and lows, upbeats and quiet notes, all the while stirring my soul. I closed my eyes and felt the music reach places in my heart I didn't know were closed.

My heart ached and I could no longer contain my emotions. Tears slowly streamed down my cheeks as my senses became overwhelmed with the beauty of what I was hearing.

There I was in Prague…sitting where others had sat hundreds of years ago…listening to music from another time…

All too soon it was over. They left the stage, and I realized that not one word had been spoken that entire evening. No one introduced the artists, no one announced the next song, no one said a thing. They didn't need to — the music spoke for itself.

That night in Prague, the music stirred my soul and brought me so much joy. I finally understood the quote from poet Maya Angelou:

Life is not measured by the number of breaths we take, but by the number of moments that take our breath away.

That is what travelling does for me — it shows me things that bring me joy and makes me feel alive. It's much easier to bounce back from life's curveballs when your heart is full of joyful memories.

Next Stop: Christmas in Colombia

Joy can be found anywhere, in small moments or big events. One thing that always brings me joy no matter where I am in the world is Christmas.

In 2017, I found myself spending Christmas in Medellin, Colombia. Medellin is surrounded by mountains, full of palm trees and lush green plants, with a river going through the city and a consistent spring-time climate — earning it the title of "City of Eternal Spring."

The people are friendly, and the food is delicious, but what really made me fall in love with the city was that they love Christmas as much as I do!

There are extensive light displays in every neighborhood, much bigger than anything I've seen at home. Nearly every house and apartment building was decorated, fireworks took place every night in December, and Christmas music proudly played in stores, offices and streets.

We heard about a holiday parade taking place on Friday night and headed out. We arrived just in time to see a marching band, including flag bearers and gymnasts, performing under thousands of strings of lights. We followed along, clapping and singing and taking photos.

I couldn't stop looking around. There were families and children enjoying the festivities, food trucks and stalls with Christmas cakes and cookies, street vendors selling toys and whistles, and lights everywhere.

We followed the path and discovered lights hanging from trees, lights in the shape of cupcakes and candy canes and hot air balloons, lights covering the grass and river, lights on the fence and street posts, lights, lights and more lights!

I smiled and laughed and giggled as we strolled along. I couldn't get enough of the Christmas spirit. People asked me to take photos of them and I asked others to take photos of me.

Why is everyone so much more friendly at Christmas time?

I realized we were making a circle around a lake and in the middle was a big stage and light show set to Christmas music. I stopped to soak it all up — the lights, the music, the night sky, the people surrounding me.

When we finally decided to head home, we couldn't find an Uber or taxi. There were thousands of people, too many vehicles, and roads closed for the parade.

As we stood there waiting, our toes started tapping and we realized we were grooving to the music pouring out of a nearby bar. We decided to go in for one drink and then try to find a ride home.

We walked over and sat down on the chairs outside. People were standing around, cooking over an open fire and setting off fireworks in the street.

An older gentleman brought over four beers and set them on our table. I tried to explain that I didn't drink beer, and he directed me to a fully stocked cooler inside the front door.

As I went over to see what they had, I realized there was a bedroom across the hall...and a living room...and...wait a minute.

We were in someone's house. It wasn't a bar at all!

We had just walked up and sat down at someone's house, and they served us drinks and food — as guests. Patricia and I laughed at our mistake as they warmly included us in the festivities.

The older gentleman invited us to dance, and we took our turns dancing and laughing and watching the family celebrate.

We said our goodbyes and hopped into a taxi, marveling at the generosity of strangers and the random adventures that happen when you say "Yes."

Making ourselves comfortable at the house we thought was a bar! Medellin, Colombia

Park Arvi, Medellin, Colombia   Christmas in Colombia

Paragliding in Medellin, Colombia

Christmas in Colombia

The Get Bendy lesson here is to find what brings you joy, and joy will help carry you through.

Get Bendy Reflection Questions

Ask yourself:
- What went well today?
- What is one thing I'm looking forward to?
- Is there someone or something that always brings a smile to my face?
- What positive changes have I noticed about myself lately?

Get Bendy Exercise

Joy can be found in the small everyday things or the big life changing dreams. Look around and see what might bring you joy today.

Choose a positive affirmation or mantra and repeat it to yourself a few times. Examples include "I am capable," "Today was a good day," or "I am grateful for the small joys in life."

Chapter 4

FEEL THE FEELS

"Don't cry because it's over. Smile because it happened."

Dr. Seuss

Feeling the feels is really about acceptance. It's saying, "It is what it is." We're not fighting against it. We're not trying to change it. We're just being still in the moment and being present and accepting it for what it is. It's acceptance that helps you to find that lasting joy and happiness.

Resilience isn't about pretending everything is okay. Life can be overwhelming sometimes. The key is to find what makes you happy and what you're looking for. For me, it's travel but it won't be the same for everyone.

If you're in a situation where you're not happy, stop and take a moment. Ask yourself why you're not happy. What's going on? Is it a job, a relationship, your financial situation? And start by accepting where you're at. Don't pretend or try to ignore the problem, because life is real. There are problems in life. There are challenges, there are uncertainties. But if you can just feel that feeling, you can be guided on the path to where to go next.

61

When I left on Remote Year, I had started my own company, secured several contracts and was excited to be self-employed and in control of how much money I made. It was going to be amazing. I was going to pay off some debts, fund this adventure and return home with money in the bank.

But that's not how it worked out.

Facing the Reality of Money

I ended up coming home significantly in debt. I left with some debt, but I was confident I was going to make so much money with my new business, I would pay everything off.

Instead, I got even more in debt. When you're traveling, it's easy to say, "When am I going to be here again? I have to go do this thing. I have to go on this side trip. I have to experience this thing."

And I did all the things. I went parasailing in Colombia and in a hot air balloon over the ruins in Mexico City. I drove to the Black Sea and dipped my toes in. I went to Austria "for the weekend," and did a river cruise in Budapest. I wanted to experience everything I could.

I learned that shifting from being an employee to being self-employed was hard. You had to find the work, do the work, invoice for the work, follow up to collect payment for the work and keep new work coming in! The income I had projected was not realistic at the time and I started relying on credit cards to make up the difference each month.

I returned home in April 2018, having maxed out four credit cards and a line of credit, and depleted my Registered Retirement Savings Plan (RRSP) savings. I owed $111,833.

I had no regrets, absolutely no regrets. When I was out there, I was conscious of what I was doing and thought, "I am young enough. I can recover from this. I will be able to pay this off. It's okay." I kept telling myself, "It's okay. I'll figure this out when I get home."

Back to My Same Life, Completely Changed

I got home and if you recall, my company had held my job for me. And thank goodness they did. I was so grateful to walk into a job and start getting a paycheck every two weeks.

But I had just spent a year in total freedom. I chose what time to wake up, I chose what to do with my day, I chose where to go, I chose what to eat. It was all within my control, everything. Now I had to be at this office at a set time, and I had to stay until a specific time, even if there wasn't any work to do. And my office had no windows, so I had no natural light. I couldn't see if it was raining or sunny. I had no idea what was happening outside.

Like a plant, I started to slowly wilt. I became more and more sad every day. I'd lost my freedom. I'd lost my ability to go outside whenever I wanted, to take a three-hour lunch, or sit at the beach and listen to the waves in the middle of the day. Now somebody controlled my time. Yes, I was grateful for the job, but it came at a high cost to my mental health.

I was sitting in my office one day, trying to figure out my finances. "I'm more than $100,000 in debt and here's my paycheck. After taxes, I can put this much toward my debt. I am never going to get this paid off. Never," I cried.

Interest rates on the credit cards were 19 per cent. I was just making the interest payments, and it was a vicious cycle. I couldn't see a way out.

Epiphany and a Way Out

I left the office in the middle of the day and drove to the Kelowna cemetery, which was only a few minutes away. I walked out amongst all the tombstones and laid down in the middle. I thought, *What does it feel like to be dead?*

The only way I could see out of my problem was to just call it quits. And I thought, *Is this how I really feel?* I laid there in the grass between the tombstones and I sobbed.

The great thing about cemeteries is nobody questions you when you're crying. It's a great place to go cry if you need a big cry. What I needed to do was really feel the feels. To get uncomfortable, sit in that place and let my whole body feel the full strength of my emotions.

I laid there and I thought, *What would it feel like if I didn't exist anymore? What would that look like?* And it was heavy, and it was hard.

I laid there for a couple hours crying and thinking, *I can't work in an office with no windows. I can't have someone tell me where*

I need to be every minute of the day. I need to be free, I need to be in control of my day and my time and my choices. But I'm not in control – everything is out of control. I'm in so much debt and I'm never going to get out of debt. It's hopeless. If I can't even control my finances, how can I control anything else? Was is the point of it all?

I wanted to make my feelings as big as possible, to imagine the worst possible thing, and then see what came out of it. And what came out of it was a strong desire to live, a rallying cry of, "I've got this! I've got places to go and people to meet and this is not the end. This feels insurmountable. I have no idea how to get out of this and I'm going to need help."

I got up and went home. I was exhausted, but there was a tiny spark of hope.

I've always been independent and proud that I could figure things out on my own. But lying there, I knew I *couldn't* figure it out. I had gotten myself into the mess, but I did not know how to get out. "I have no idea what to do!" This was a new feeling for me, and I realized I had hit my rock bottom.

This is it, I thought. *I'm here, I'm feeling it all. I'm feeling overwhelmed and distraught and uncertain about my future.* But as soon as I really allowed myself to feel, I knew I wasn't uncertain about my future. I knew I wanted to have a future. I just didn't know how to get there. And so that's when I started asking for help from people who had done what I wanted to do, people who had gotten themselves out of debt and knew how to guide me, and knew each step to take to get out of debt.

And I'm so grateful to them, but I'm also really proud of myself that I allowed myself to feel all my emotions, because it would have been easy just to sit in my office and pout, "This sucks," and not acknowledge the depths of despair I was feeling. Because it's scary to go into those dark places. It's scary because you wonder if you're going to get out. I didn't know. But I thought, *Feel the feels, get bendy. Let yourself feel whatever emotion it is that you're feeling. That's part of living, to experience all the emotions. It's not all sunshine and roses. It's not, and that's okay.*

Fear and Ecstasy: Journey to the South Pole

Feeling the feels is about feeling all the emotions — good and bad — and knowing you'll be okay. When you travel, you can experience a full range of emotions in one day.

In January 2011, I was heading to Antarctica — basically the bottom of the world. My travel plans saw me fly from Kelowna (British Columbia, Canada) to Calgary to Houston to Buenos Aires and finally Ushuaia, Argentina. Total travel time was 27 hours, if I made all my connections.

My connecting flight in Buenos Aires meant transferring from the international airport to the domestic airport. As I walked through the airport and outside, a heat wave washed over me. I had started my day in snow and cold, and now I was in full sunshine and humidity.

Confidently strolling through the airport like a seasoned traveller, I walked to the taxi lineup and was instantly surrounded by men pulling me in every direction to get into their cab. I pushed on, walking toward what I thought was a taxi stand and assistance for agreeing to a set rate. It was empty. I turned around and a nice man said, "Hey lady, where you want to go?" I told him I needed to go to the domestic airport. "No problem, hop in."

I got into the back of the cab, reached for my seatbelt and found it was stuck. He had already zipped away from the curb, so I pulled harder. The seatbelt flew out of the wall and struck me in the face. Ouch! Right between the eyes, opening a cut with blood now trickling down the side of my nose. Okay, not the best start — I'm bleeding and I don't have a seatbelt on. My driver is flying along, asking me questions in a combination of English and Spanish. I pick out every fourth or fifth word and we somewhat manage a conversation.

Traffic was busy but that didn't slow us down. We cruised along as I got my first glimpse of Buenos Aires. He pointed out landmarks and told me their history. It looked like an interesting city, and I settled back to take in the views.

Suddenly, we were leaving the highway and entering a residential area. Where were we going? My heart started to beat a bit faster — I'm alone and although I'm expected in Ushuaia, it would be hours before anyone knew I was missing.

We pulled up to a house and the driver got out, taking my suitcase out of the trunk. "What's happening?" I ask. He gestured for me to stay in the car, and he went inside the house. Stray dogs were strolling the streets, and I felt vulnerable.

Two men exited the house, picked up my suitcase and put it in another car. "Get in." Ummm, okay. Now we're in a new car but it's the same driver. I'm still nervous and had no idea why we stopped but trust we're carrying on to the airport.

A few blocks down the road, we pull into a gas station, the driver gets out and disappears. Now what? Do I stay in the back of this random car or get out? If I get out, where do I go?

Panic slowly started to rise as I dug for my cell phone and hoped to have service, although I'm not sure who I was going to call. The driver returned with two open bottles of Coke and offered me one. "No thanks," I said. "Please take me to the airport." He got back in the car and we continued on our way.

Now we're back on the highway and driving way too fast. I mean really fast. I asked him to slow down and he started laughing — Mario Andretti," he said, pointing to himself. Oh great, I'm in a strange car with a man who thinks he's a race car driver. I see flashes of the headlines: "Canadian girl killed in car crash in Buenos Aires." How ironic, as I'd spent my career raising awareness about road safety.

We zigged and zagged through traffic, my driver only laughing harder at the obvious terror in my eyes. *Please let me make it the airport alive,* I thought.

Finally, he pulled over to the side of the road and said, "Airport there," pointing across six lanes of highway traffic. "No, take me to the airport, not near it," I said. After some back and forth, he finally sped across traffic to drop me off in the airport parking lot. I'd never been so happy to get out of a car.

The rest of the journey was happily uneventful, and I arrived in Ushuaia tired, sweaty and ready to lie down. I boarded the cruise ship and quickly fell asleep.

Rough Water and Penguin Paradise

We had a two-day sailing across the Drake Passage between Cape Horn, Chile and Antarctica, some of the roughest water in the world, and it lived up to its reputation. I spent most of the time clinging to the bed as the ship went up and then crashed down over the swells.

But then we arrived, officially entering the Antarctic Circle, and took Zodiacs to step onto the continent. We were at Brown Bluff, the sun was shining, and I sat on a rock surrounded by thousands of Gentoo penguins. It was magical, and it felt like I was on another planet. The air was fresh and clean, the water was clear and cold, and the sky was huge. There were no roads, no planes, no buildings, no people. It was peaceful and surreal.

As the days went by, I fell more in love with Antarctica. Its unspoiled beauty, its quiet stillness, its unending views. Time seemed to stand still, and I felt my whole body relax. It was a place to recharge, to unwind and reflect on life.

The range of emotions I felt — from fear that I was being kidnapped, to exhaustion from 27 hours of travel, to pure joy at seeing so many penguins up close — I fully experienced it all.

Penguins in the Antarctic

Exploring Antarctica by Zodiac

Antarctica

Antarctica

Penguins in Antarctica

I love penguins! Antarctica

The Get Bendy lesson here is to allow yourself to feel whatever emotion you're feeling.

Get Bendy Reflection Questions

Ask yourself:

- What aspects of myself or my life have I found the hardest to accept, and why?
- How does practicing acceptance impact my overall well-being and sense of peace?
- Am I holding onto something I need to let go of?
- What am I really scared of?
- If this were the last day of my life, would I have the same plans for today?

Get Bendy Exercise

Write down your fears or anxieties. Make them bigger. Write down the worst possible scenario. Now sit there. Sit in that space surrounded by the worst possible scenario you could think of. How does it feel? What comes up?

Once you face the darkest place you can imagine, it is no longer unknown, and you'll find your fear subside. You'll likely also find the answer you need to take the next step.

Chapter 5

RALLY THE TROOPS

"Alone, we can do so little; together, we can do so much."

Helen Keller

allying the troops is one of the keys to bouncing back. You can't bounce back by yourself every time. From some of the smaller things in life, absolutely, you can bounce back and figure that out on your own. But the big things, when you're in financial distress like I was, or you're getting a health diagnosis that you weren't expecting, you need support.

Rallying the troops is about being vulnerable, it's about asking for help. It's finding the people that can help you get through to the other side, to bounce back from whatever life has thrown at you.

My big issue was the financial crisis I incurred during my travel adventure with Remote Year in 2017. I thought starting my own business would cover all my expenses plus pay off past debts, but instead I went further into debt with each month that passed. Rallying helped me move forward.

I didn't know how to get out of debt. I knew I needed help, but I was embarrassed. I heard about a networking event called "Women in Business" and decided to go. I sat in the parking lot for almost half an hour working up the nerve to go inside and meet new people. My desire to get out of debt was stronger than my aversion to being uncomfortable so I made myself a deal — all I had to do was meet two people. Once I talked to two people, then I could go home. That seemed manageable so I walked in.

As soon as I walked through the door, a lovely woman greeted me and said, "Hi, I'm Chantal Diaz, what do you do?" We chatted for a few minutes, and I learned she was a financial advisor. I took a deep breath and summoned as much courage as possible and said, "I'm over $100,000 in debt and I have no idea how to get out." Chantal smiled and said, "Perfect, I love helping women figure this out!"

There was no judgment, there was no, "How did you get here? You should know better." There was none of that. She simply said, "Come to my office. We're going to make a game plan."

And then Chantal introduced me to another woman, Meaghan, and we totally hit it off. So, within the first five minutes, I had met two amazing people, and I honored the deal with myself and left the event. I went home feeling proud of myself for getting out there, being vulnerable and asking for help.

A Plan for Getting Out of Debt

I set up an appointment with Chantal and she spent the afternoon going through all my financial information, reviewing the terms on my credit cards and lines of credit, looking at my insurance policies and pension plan, and the terms of my mortgage. We agreed the only goal was to get out of debt — we could look at investing and saving down the road.

Chantal gave me a list of homework and I committed to complete each item on the list. Some items were small, like calling all my providers and asking for a better rate. I phoned my Internet and cellphone providers, and both switched me to more affordable plans.

I also canceled any monthly subscriptions that weren't critical (no more Spotify or Netflix). Some items felt bigger, like phoning my credit card companies and asking them to lower my rate. I phoned and didn't have any luck but kept working my way down my homework list.

One of the bigger items involved a complete mindset shift. Chantal advised me to only pay cash for everything. And no, that doesn't mean using a debit card. When you tap a plastic card, there's no connection to what it actually costs. But when you hand over a $50 bill, you're very aware. There's a feeling in your body and it might even make you stop to think about how you want to spend your money.

I didn't have a budget — I could decide whatever budget I wanted — but the key was to only pay cash for everyday items. Things like my mortgage and car payment and insurance were fixed costs set up on autopay through the bank. But everything else needed to be cash — groceries, gas, haircut, gifts, eating out, vitamins, dry cleaning, etc.

Chantal said to pick a number that I thought I needed each week (I chose $250), and then go to the bank and take out that much money for the month ($1,000). Then take the cash and divide it into four envelopes, one envelope for each week of the month. On Sunday, you pull out "Week one" envelope, put that cash in your wallet and that's what you use for the week. You can use it however you want and when the money in your wallet is gone, that's it until Sunday when you can pull out the "Week two" envelope.

It took some getting used to only using the cash in my wallet, but I learned to love it. It's certainly more convenient to tap your card when filling up your car with gas and now I had to go into the store, wait in line, pay cash and then go back to fill my car. But I became more aware of how much I actually spent. Some weeks I ran out of money on Thursday or Friday, and other weeks I still had money left over (which I called my "bonus" money).

The process was empowering. For example, I saw a pair of cozy pajama bottoms for $20. Previously, I would have just grabbed them, tapped my card and carried on. Now I stopped and looked in my wallet. I had $25 left for the week. I got to choose – I could get the pajamas, or I could go out with friends for happy hour after work. It didn't matter what I chose, it was the fact that I got to choose (which feels empowering), and I felt a connection to my money (which helped me heal).

Baby Steps, Then Leveling Up

I bought myself a wallet that felt beautiful so every time I pulled it out, I would feel abundant. I spent the next several months following this process of all cash for everything. And it really helped: My spending went down (without feeling like I was on a "budget"), and I started connecting to my money in a positive way.

As I reported back to Chantal with my progress, she coached me on tackling the high-interest credit cards. I started applying for credit cards that offered zero per cent interest with balance transfers, so I could transfer balances from my higher interest credit cards and focus on paying one card down without accruing interest. I would put every spare dollar onto that card until it was paid off, then I would repeat the process on the next one.

I was making progress, but it was still going to take a long time to be debt free. I needed to up my game and get more serious. I reached out to my friend Chris and offered to take him for lunch. Chris is in real estate and so much more. He loves helping people and coming up with creative solutions. And I felt safe telling him all the details of my financial situation.

He listened and said, "Okay, how uncomfortable do you want to get? How committed are you to this?" And I said, "This is the only thing I want, to get out of debt. I want to be debt free come hell or high water." And he said, "Okay, you could Airbnb your second bedroom." And I said, "Oh, I don't want strangers in my condo." "Okay, you could get a roommate." "Oh, no, I like my independence." He laughed, "How bad do you want this?"

He was right. I said I was committed. I said this was the only thing that mattered right now so I needed to seriously look at all the options, even if it made me uncomfortable.

I decided I would rent out my whole condo, and I would offer to housesit elsewhere. This felt like a great solution to save money and have my own space. The rent would cover my mortgage, and then the money I would have been paying for mortgage would go toward paying down the debt.

I shared this idea with a few people, and they all thought I was crazy. "Good luck. Where are you going to find a house-sitting gig?" But that didn't stop me — I was used to people thinking my ideas were crazy. I believed in me, and I was going to make it happen.

Manifesting the Plan

I'm sure you've heard of manifestation. If you haven't, manifestation, according to dictionary.com, is *the act or practice of trying to attain something desired by thinking about or focusing on it.* Any thought, goal or idea that you can hold in your conscious mind on a continuing basis and that you intensely desire or intensely fear, must be brought into reality. Whether positive or negative, good or bad, if you hold it continuously, emotionalize it, and visualize it in your conscious mind, the Superconscious Mind will begin to organize the entire universe of experience around you to draw into your life the people and circumstances necessary to make that idea come true.

The next night, my lifelong friends Tammy and Curtis invited me out to their cabin for dinner. As we were sitting there looking at the lake, I told them about my housesitting idea. They both looked at me and I thought they were about to say the same thing as everyone else, but instead they said, "Our neighbour just asked us today if we knew anyone who could house sit because he got a job offer in Abu Dhabi. They're leaving on Saturday, and they want someone to take care of their house for a year."

Wow, *that* is the power of manifestation! I had an idea, I committed to it, I felt it strongly, I visualized it and the Universe delivered. The Universe brought me the exact people and circumstances I needed to fulfill my desire to housesit and pay down debt.

I met the owners on Friday, and we hit it off. Their house was stunning. It was the former show home for the area that was being developed. With my friends vouching for me and their plane leaving the next day, the deal was done quickly and they handed me the keys.

I was in a flow state — that sense of fluidity between your body and mind, where you are totally absorbed by and deeply focused on something and nothing can distract you. When you can maintain that focus and stability of mind, miracles happen. The Universe acts with speed and urgency when there is alignment, when your thoughts and actions are completely aligned with your goal.[2]

I got to live next door to my best friend in a mansion — three-story house, big backyard, bright windows, two-car garage — and I didn't even have to clean it. The owners had a housekeeper who came once a month. They also covered all the utilities including Internet and Netflix. I was simply living in the house, bringing in the mail and making sure nothing went wrong. All while exploring a new neighborhood, living next to my best friend and not paying a dime.

---

2 (https://www.headspace.com/articles/flow-state)

And in the meantime, I rented out my condo to a guy who was thrilled to be there. So, my mortgage was getting paid, I was significantly paying down debt and living a lifestyle I hadn't even imagined. That's how powerful manifestation can be when you get clear on the end goal.

I rallied the troops, from my best friend and her neighbor to the financial advisor I met at a networking event (who went on to become a dear friend), and other friends who challenged me on how bad I wanted it. I had their support and expertise and guidance — it made all the difference.

With hard work, commitment and a team of support, I was debt free in two years and three months.

My housesitting gig

Key steps to get out of debt

- Get clear on why you want to be debt free and commit to your goal.
- Ask for help from someone who's done what you want to do.
- Start paying cash – use the weekly envelope system.
- Apply for zero interest credit cards and transfer higher interest balances.
- Call all your service companies and ask for better rates (e.g. Internet, cell phone).
- Cancel subscriptions.
- Try batch cooking to help save on groceries.
- Look at leasing versus buying a vehicle.
- Understand your debt: Write down exactly how much you owe on each card and the interest rate.
- Understand your credit score, how it's calculated and how you can improve it (ask for help if needed).
- Get creative: Could you get a roommate, take in a student, rent your place and live free somewhere (housesit, stay with family or friends), start a side-business, take on a part-time job.

Learning to Ask for Help

Life can present all sorts of opportunities to practice resilience. A financial crisis is just one scenario in which you might want to lean on friends and experts to help. For many, it's an unexpected health diagnosis. Or it could be the end of a marriage, the loss of a job, the death of a loved one. We are not meant to carry these burdens alone and learning to ask, and receive, help can be hard, but it gets easier with practice.

The Next Step: Physical Fine Tuning

After my success rallying the troops to get out of debt, I found it much easier to ask for help in other areas of my life. When I was in my early 20s, I was diagnosed with a condition known as Charcot Marie Tooth (CMT – the last names of the three physicians who described it in 1886) — a disease of the peripheral nerves. The peripheral nerves connect the brain to the rest of the body and allow the brain to send messages to the body while also allowing the body to send messages to the brain. Over time, CMT causes these messages to slow down, resulting in challenges with balance and frequent falls.

At first, I was delighted to realize I wasn't clumsy! I fell so much as a child that my knees were permanently scarred. Running and most sports were difficult for me, and I thought I simply wasn't athletic. Learning there was an actual reason for why I fell, for why my ankles rolled without warning, was empowering. But then learning there was no treatment or cure was a letdown. I basically chose to ignore the diagnosis and carry on with the care-free lifestyle of a 20-something.

As I got older, I started to notice changes — I couldn't wear high heels anymore, I couldn't walk down a flight of stairs without holding the handrail, I fatigued easily while walking. I finally decided to accept the fact that I might need help. Even though there was no treatment, perhaps there were things I could do to slow down the process.

I started talking to people I knew and trusted. I shared with my friend and massage therapist, Jen. She was amazing and started focusing a part of each session on my feet. She worked on my toes and my ankles and my calves, trying to open up the neural pathways again. Sometimes I felt nothing and other times I felt shooting pain; any type of feeling was a good sign in my opinion.

Jen asked if I was seeing a chiropractor, and I said "No." She said I had to go see her friend Matt — he was a chiropractor and so much more. I made an appointment with Matt and he amazed me. He was the first person I met who actually knew what CMT was! He said they learned about it at school, but he had never met anyone with the condition. He was eager to work with me and developed a series of exercises for me to do at home, with support from him along the way. After each session with him, I walked away feeling hopeful and a bit lighter.

Matt asked who I was seeing to support my nutrition, as food and supplements play a key role in healing the body. He suggested I see his colleague Brittany, a naturopath, and I booked in right away. Brittany did a series of tests, including genetic testing, and discovered some unique needs and deficiencies. She put together a supplement plan and helped with a meal plan that was simple yet effective for me.

Things were coming together, and I was feeling better every day, but I wanted more. Matt suggested I add in personal training — someone with whom he could share information, so the exercises would align with the work he was doing. He got me in to see

Taylor, a highly sought-after personal trainer and co-owner of a women's-only gym.

Taylor set me up with a program, which she tweaked after each session I had with Matt. She understood my limitations and what we were trying to achieve and developed a program to target those specific needs.

Jen, Matt, Brittany and Taylor all shared information about me. They reported back on my progress and challenges, they brainstormed new things to try, they shared research on CMT. Without realizing it, I had created a team. A team of health care professionals dedicated to helping me succeed. I felt inspired and cared for and strong.

Harnessing the power of experts and asking for help is the best way to move through any crisis. I still have CMT, and I still have challenges with stairs and balance, but I have a team supporting me, cheering me on and believing in me. That makes it easier to stay positive and see all the good things in my life.

The Get Bendy lesson here is to ask for help and be open to receive.

Get Bendy Reflection Questions

Ask yourself:
- What does community mean to me, and how do I experience it in my life?
- What challengers or barriers have I faced in building or maintaining a sense of community?

- What matters most in my life?
- Is there a part of my life where I'm struggling? (Finances, relationship, health, career, etc.) What would life look like if I didn't struggle with that part anymore?

Get Bendy Exercise

Write down one area of your life in which you could use some help.

Next, who do you know who has achieved what you'd like to achieve? It could be someone at work, a friend, or even a celebrity.

Reach out to that person and ask if you can connect. With a friend or co-worker, it could mean going for a coffee or lunch. With a celebrity, it might look like joining their email list or buying their book or signing up for a program they offer. Start to talk about where you're at and where you'd like to be. Ask them how they did it and if they'd be willing to mentor you.

If you don't know anyone, start asking around! Ask your friends, your hairdresser, your waitress — everyone you come into contact with — if they know anyone with experience in the thing you want. It might mean going to a networking event and getting out of your comfort zone. But if you want to change an area of your life, once you commit, you'll find the right people and opportunities will appear.

Chapter 6

CHOOSE YOUR ADVENTURE

"It's not what happens to you, but how you react to it that matters."

Epictetus

Remember those children's books where you were the protagonist and basically wrote the story? Travel is the ultimate "choose your own adventure" story. You constantly get to choose which destination is next, how you're going to get there, where you're going to stay, what you're going to eat. Of course, none of these plans will work out exactly as you thought, so you also get to choose how to respond. The choice is yours — you can **react**, or you can **respond**.

Reacting is immediate. It's automatic and you don't really think about it, while responding is taking a minute, thinking, and then taking action.

Again, the choice is yours. But responding is a much happier way to live. It's much more easeful, going with the flow, and it's a more deliberate way to live. And it uses a different part of your brain than being reactive. Being reactionary is based more in your amygdala, the part of your temporal lobe that acts as a processing centre for emotions. And response is in the prefrontal cortex, your personality centre, so it involves really seeing your options, choosing how you're going to respond, how you're going to meet this moment.

I remember the first time in my life that I deliberately paused and responded instead of reacting. I'm not sure if it comes with maturity or practice, or both. But I was in a wonderful relationship and head over heels in love.

Tough Lesson: The Big Romantic Getaway

We met in 2010 and had been together for almost five years. With our five-year anniversary coming up, and a big birthday for me, we decided to do something special and celebrate in Hawaii.

As a traveler and lover of new experiences, this may sound funny, but I've purposely not traveled to specific destinations because I've been "saving them" for a special occasion. Some people save the fancy dishes or save the sexy lingerie, but I save cities and countries. Paris, France and Hawaii are my two "special spots," and I wanted to experience them with someone I love.

He said, "It will be too rainy and cold in Paris this time of year, so let's do Hawaii." I reminded him I was saving Hawaii for something really romantic. And he replied, "What's more romantic than our five-year anniversary and your 40th birthday?" Sounded pretty romantic, so I said, "Let's go!"

We planned to spend two weeks in Maui. We rented a beautiful condo, booked a convertible rental car and made reservations at a fancy restaurant, Mama's Fish House. Everyone was convinced he was going to propose, and I thought so, too.

We had talked about getting married. We discussed our future and it seemed he was trying hard to plan a really romantic trip for me. I was excited — we were going to start our next chapter together. I had always wanted to be married and here was a wonderful man, who I loved, my family loved, my friends loved, and he loved me. We had had amazing travel adventures together and seemed aligned in what we wanted for the future.

As I'm packing for Maui, those were my expectations — I'm going to Hawaii to get engaged. As we're getting ready to head out the door, he says, "I can't do this." "What?" I responded. "You can't get that bag closed? You forgot your passport?" He says, "No, I can't do this relationship."

Ummm, what?

Time stopped. The world stopped. There was no sound. I stood there, frozen in place.

"Pardon?" was all I could manage.

"I'm sorry, I can't be in this relationship anymore," he whispered.

We're about to spend two romantic weeks together in Maui, we're about to get engaged, we're taking the next step in our relationship. Aren't we?

I stood there and thought, *The only thing I can control is my reaction. I could lose my mind here right now. I could scream, I could throw things, I could cry. What do I want to do?*

And I had a flash of clarity: Take a moment.

I didn't need to do anything. I didn't need to say anything. I could simply "take a moment" and then choose an action.

So I said, "Just give me a moment," and I went into the bathroom and turned on the shower. Water is very soothing for me, so I stood there in the shower, in shock as I tried to comprehend the last few minutes. "The love of my life has just told me he doesn't want to be with me anymore. And he's given me no reason. And I didn't see this coming." Let's process that for a minute.

And then I thought, *Okay, what are my choices here?*

Option one is I don't go, I cancel the trip. But then I lose all the money on the deposit for the condo, it's too late to get a refund on the flights or the car rental. And then I have to go back to work and explain he broke up with me instead of getting engaged. That sucks. Nope, not a great option.

Option two is I go by myself. And I say to him, 'See you later. You're out of here. I'm going to go and have this trip alone.'" Well, the car rental is in his name, so how is that going to work? And do I want to be in Hawaii by myself for two weeks with a broken heart? That sucks too.

Option three is we go and make the best of it. As I stood there in the shower, option three seemed like the best choice. So, I got dressed, came out and said, "We're going to go. I don't want to talk about it. Let's just go and try to have a good time."

I think he was expecting me to be a mess, to fall apart, to scream or cry. And I was calm. I was so calm.

I kept telling myself, "All I can do is choose how to respond in this moment. How do I want to respond to this information?" And I thought, *I want to be calm. I want to feel peace. I'm not going to stand here trying to convince him to be with me. I'm also not going to throw away this dream trip that we've already paid for. So let's go.*

Making the Best of a Weird Situation

We went and for the most part, it was pretty good. We went on a whale-watching tour, we drove the road to Hana, and we explored beaches. We strolled along the beach every night to watch the sunset. We swam in the pool; we made dinner and we laughed.

We got up in the middle of the night and drove to Haleakalā to watch the sunrise. It was ridiculously cold, like we've never been so cold in our lives. We wore all the clothes that we had. We even took a blanket off the bed, and we were wrapped up together at the top of the volcano to watch the sunrise. We were laughing and laughing, because it was so hot during the day, we never imagined it could be so cold. But the sunrise was magical and I'm so happy to have shared that moment together.

We kept the reservation at Mama's Fish House, and they totally spoiled me and brought me wonderful desserts and sang "Happy Birthday" to me. I remember thinking at times, *We're so good together. Why would you want to break up?* But I didn't say anything, I just let him make his choice.

We flew home, he packed up his things and the next morning he drove away. And I've never seen him again.

I learned so many things about myself in that relationship and one of the best gifts was choosing how I wanted to handle things in the end. And ever since, it's been a defining moment in my brain. When new, unexpected things come at me now, I confidently say, "I'll get back to you." And know I don't have to answer right away.

Knowing I don't have to respond instantly has brought me so much peace and comfort.

I'm sure we've all had our hearts broken at some point. And maybe we didn't always handle it with grace. I know I haven't. But in this case, I was proud of how I handled it. It was a defining moment for me in learning about resilience and taking the control I could in my own life.

That's when, if you are aware of that feeling, you just let it go and watch it travel through.

Mama's Fish House, Maui, Hawaii

Sunrise at Haleakala National Park, Maui

Maui, Hawaii

High Altitude Life Lessons

As tough as that heartbreaking choice was to make, some adventures are easy choices that lead to unexpected results. When I saw that my Remote Year itinerary included Peru, I began planning a side trip to Machu Picchu. I didn't realize all the ways you could arrive there — everything from one-, two-, and four-day hikes, the classic Inca Trail, the short Inca Trail, the Salcantay/Inca Trail combo and more.

As I read about the effects of high altitudes and was honest about my current level of fitness, I decided the best route for me was to take a train, then a bus, and then explore the actual ruins.

CHOOSE YOUR ADVENTURE

Five girlfriends and I boarded a plane in Lima and took the 1-hour, 15-minute flight to Cusco.

Although I typically don't take medicine unless absolutely necessary, I gave in to my friends' concern and took an altitude sickness pill before landing. (Cusco's elevation is 3,400 m or 11,200 ft.)

We checked into our hotel and headed off to find lunch. As we walked along, we noticed we were all short of breath and our energy was low. We stopped at a nearby restaurant to give ourselves time to acclimatize.

Part way through our meal, one of our friends pushed her plate back and said she wasn't feeling well. All the color drained from her face and we barely caught her as she passed out.

Our waiter came over quickly and began fanning her, another staff person brought some rubbing alcohol and slowly our friend came to. But then, just as quickly, her color faded again, but this time her lips turned blue and she started convulsing.

I've never been so terrified in my life.

We got her on the floor, one person called International SOS to find us a hospital, someone else called a taxi, someone paid our bill and I grabbed all her belongings. We got her into the cab, two friends jumped in with her and they sped off.

Adrienne and I stood on the sidewalk shaking like little leaves.

What just happened?

Was that altitude sickness?

Could it happen to us at any moment?

We showed each other where we kept our medical insurance cards, confirmed we both had the SOS app on our phones and made a plan in case one of us passed out.

Then we slowly walked to the textile museum to check out the ancient art of weaving, and hopefully calm ourselves down.

Eight hours later, the hospital released our friend and gave her permission to carry on to Aguas Caliente, which is a lower altitude. She had high-altitude cerebral edema (HACE) — a life-threatening form of altitude sickness where your brain swells when you reach high altitudes. The oxygen level at high altitudes is less than what your body knows as normal. As a result, your brain reacts negatively to the lack of oxygen by swelling. The pressure of your brain against your skull is dangerous and affects how your body functions. HACE affects less than one percent of people who reach an altitude above 4,000 meters and is the least common form of altitude sickness. If treated quickly, the risk of developing long-term effects is low.

Exhausted and relieved, we boarded the train for our 4.5-hour journey to Aguas Caliente (aka Machu Picchu). The train ride was stunning, with a full glass roof so we could see all the mountains, rivers, valleys and towns.

Too excited to sleep in, we were standing in line at 5am waiting to be whisked up the mountain to get our first glimpse of Machu Picchu.

The bus ride may seem like the easy choice compared to the steep climb up, but it had its own element of danger. The drivers roared up the mountain like race car drivers, fish-tailing the bus around each switchback, and leaving us hanging on to the seats for dear life. The dirt road is only wide enough for one bus in most spots, although we somehow squeezed by when an approaching bus came barreling downhill.

With no guard rails and a long way down, I kept my eyes on the horizon and the sunshine hitting the peaks of the mountains.

Twenty minutes later, we got off the bus and joined the line to enter the main gates.

Our guide led us along the path and made a quick left up a series of stone steps, climbing higher and higher. Some stairs were a small step up, while others were a big step up and required a helping hand from friends.

Finally, we were at the top. I walked around the corner and there it was — the Machu Picchu you see in all the photos. Only more beautiful in person.

The sun was shining, the sky was blue and all of Machu Picchu laid out before me in lush greens and smooth sand-colored rocks. It was breath-taking.

I stood there and stared. I breathed in the fresh mountain air and marveled at the series of events that led me to be standing in this very place. The dreams you have, the planning you do, and then the moment it all comes together. It's magical.

Of course we took hundreds of photos: photos of Machu Picchu, photos of just me, photos of our group. We carried on for three hours, our guide explaining the history, the culture, the purposes for each section of the citadel, the perfect placement of windows and rocks to line up with the sun and stars. It was fascinating.

Then our group divided, half deciding to climb Machu Picchu Mountain (four hours of gruelling stone stairs) and the other half continuing to explore the Machu Picchu citadel. (Guess which group I chose? Yup, no more stairs for me!)

We wandered through the ruins looking for the perfect spot to do a meditation together. Our friend had fully recovered, with no lingering side effects. We were so grateful for her health and that we were all together to share this magical experience. We found a room we hadn't explored before, sat down on rocks that seemed meant for the purpose and closed our eyes.

Warmed by the sun, lulled by a gentle breeze, I soaked up every sensation and felt my heart full of love and gratitude — for the journey, for the women I shared it with, for this beautiful place.

The next day Amy and Adrienne headed back to hike Huayna Picchu Mountain and the other girls stayed in town. I decided to head back to Machu Picchu citadel and explore more on my own.

Taking my time, I chose which path to take, found quiet places to sit and enjoy the views and made friends with the local llamas. I learned that most of the llamas on Machu Picchu are female and many of them were pregnant. How fun would it be to come back when all the babies are born?!

Waiting for Amy and Adrienne to return, I made my way to a spot beside two ladies. They told me their husbands had gone off to explore but the stairs were too difficult for them. We laughed and chatted and swapped travel stories. They were from Austria and had traveled all over the world, but this was their first time in Peru.

My friends arrived and I gave the ladies a hug goodbye, inspired by their adventurous spirits.

The next day we took the train back to Cusco, and we were fortunate to be sitting with a charming older gentleman from Denmark. He had the most beautiful smile and infectious laugh.

He was so full of life and told me that ever since he was a little boy, he had dreamed of seeing the world. At 85 years old, he was still traveling — on his own! — and planned to keep going until he couldn't walk anymore.

My trip to Machu Picchu taught me several lessons:
- It's okay to lean on friends for support, they're happy to help.
- Surround yourself with powerful women and let those friendships lift you.
- Trust your intuition — the right people will show up exactly when needed.
- The energy you put out gets returned to you.
- It's never too late to pursue a dream.
- The world is small and full of good people.

If Machu Picchu is on your bucket list, do it now! You won't be disappointed. Give yourself plenty of time, take altitude sickness medication and be prepared to feel humbled, curious and grateful.

Machu Pichu, Peru

The girls, Machu Pichu

Grateful to be together

Machu Pichu, Peru

The Get Bendy lesson here is to remember you always have a choice.

Get Bendy Reflection Questions

Ask yourself:

- "There is no good, there is no bad, there is only your perception." Is this true?
- What aspects of my life do I feel the need to control? Why?
- How does my desire to control impact my stress levels and overall well-being?
- What will I do differently next time?

Get Bendy Exercise

If you can control your perception, you get to decide if something is an opportunity or the end of the world.

Try to reframe a current situation. You may need to practice this several times before it starts to feel natural.

First, be a journalist and describe what happened, sticking to facts and no emotions.

Example: He broke up with me.

Next, write down your first response to this fact.

Example: He broke up with me and now my heart is broken and no one will ever love me again and I'll never get married and my life is ruined.

Next, and here's the fun part, see if you can reframe your initial response into an opportunity statement.

Example: He broke up with me and now I have the opportunity to reflect on where I'm going and make a different choice.

It can be hard at first but keep practicing, reframing your first reaction into an opportunity, and choose what brings you joy.

Chapter 7

LOOK INSIDE

"A woman knows by intuition, or instinct, what is best for herself."

Marilyn Monroe

I love intuition. It's a critical skill, especially as a single woman travelling. It's that voice you hear saying, "Turn here," or that feeling in your chest saying, "Yes," or a gentle nudge letting you know you're on the right path.

Intuition feels calm, an inner knowing, a certainty. It's clarifying. It's a muscle you can develop as you consistently use it. Your body always knows the answer, if you stop and tune in.

This took some time for me to learn but it really kicked in when I started traveling on my own, because you have to be aware of everything that's going on around you. And you have to listen.

The first time I clearly remember my intuition guiding me was in Barcelona. It was June 2009, and I was going on a

Mediterranean cruise with my side-business company. The ship was leaving from Barcelona, and I decided to arrive a few days early to explore.

Barcelona is a bustling city and there were lots of things happening. I strolled down the famous Las Ramblas, crowded with people and vendors and music. I decided to step away from the crowds and explore some of the old side streets. I strolled along exploring the history, popping into little stores and enjoying the evening. As I came to a cross street and was about to turn right, I heard a loud voice inside of me say, "Do not go down that street."

Why? What's wrong with the street? There were shops, and cafes, and all sorts of things to explore. It looked like any other street.

But my body would not step toward that street. The feeling was so powerful, and I thought, *I am not meant to go down that street. I'm not going to question it. I'm not going to argue with myself. I accept that this is not the street for me.*

I went down another street and wandered in and out of shops and of course nothing happened. It was a lovely adventure. I don't know what would have happened if I'd gone down that street. But I just knew — my body knew — not to go down that street. And that's when I realized your intuition is really heightened when you're travelling, and I learned to pay closer attention to my body.

Sagrada Familia, Barcelona, Spain

Beyond Logic: Meeting THE ONE

Intuition isn't about logic – you can't argue with yourself and try to rationalize why or why not you're about to take a certain action. You simply need to accept your intuition and trust yourself to know what's best for you.

From a resilience point of view, intuition is about knowing what's right for you. So, when life throws you something, you can listen to your own intuition and decide how you will respond.

I'm a romantic. I believe there's someone out there for everyone and nothing makes me happier than seeing two people in love. The trouble is, it's easy for me to fall in love. I see the good in people and I fall hard. Sometimes it turns into a fabulous love story and sometimes I get my heart broken. It's okay — I'll never regret falling in love.

I was 35 years old when I met the man I thought I'd marry. Alex (not his real name) and I met online (how else do you meet people these days?) He lived in Calgary, and I was in Kelowna, B.C., so we started with a phone date. That first call lasted several hours, and I later learned he had called me from his car in a parking lot because he hadn't made it home in time for our call. He was funny and thoughtful and easy to talk to. We made plans to talk again the next day, and the next, and the next. We were spending hours on the phone getting to know each other.

One of the great things about phone calls is you can talk about anything — you don't have to worry about awkward body language (his or yours) and if things go bad, you can just hang up. This meant we had covered every topic from marriage to kids to past relationships to future goals. We shared childhood memories, both good and bad, and I felt my heart melting more with each conversation.

We agreed it was time to meet in person but before we could make arrangements, he was called back to work early. Alex worked on a cruise ship, at sea for four months and then home for two months. Undaunted, we decided to keep talking every day and see where things went.

Two weeks and dozens of hours of talking later, I had fallen in love. I know, I know — how do you fall in love with someone you've never met? It's crazy but that's what happens when you're a romantic. And he said he felt the same way about me.

We simply couldn't wait four months until he got back for us to meet — I needed to meet him now. What if we didn't click in person? Then we would have wasted all those months having conversations and falling in love with a person we created in our minds. I didn't want to do that, so we needed a plan.

We looked at the ship's itinerary and tried to find a port that would be easy for me to fly to. Dublin, Ireland made the most sense. I could fly there, join him on the ship as he sailed the "remote islands of the UK," and fly home from London.

I arranged the time off work and booked my flights, telling no one but my sister (I tell her everything). With a retired police officer as my dad and an older brother with a temper for any guy who looked at me, I knew they wouldn't approve. I didn't even tell my friends, as I imagined them trying to talk me out of flying halfway around the world to meet a man I had only ever spoken to on the phone.

But here's the thing — I knew it was the right decision. I knew he was a good man. I knew this was a love story in the making. I felt at peace. There wasn't one ounce of doubt in my mind or body. My intuition was giving me the green light and I was going for it.

As I walked down the airport concourse, something on the ground caught my eye. I picked up the silver square and turned it over. It was a magnet that said, "Sometimes in the middle of an ordinary life, love gives us a fairy tale." How is that for a sign?!

I flew to Dublin and checked into the hotel Alex had booked for me. After a luxurious bubble bath and room service, I fell asleep. The next morning, Alex came to the hotel to pick me up. He was even more handsome in person and in uniform! His driver took us to the ship, where I boarded and was treated like royalty as his guest.

We spent nine days cruising through the UK, falling even more in love. And over the next five years, we had grand adventures as we traveled around the world. His schedule was four months on the ship, two months home. We decided four months was too long to be apart, so I flew to wherever he was at the two-month mark and spent a couple weeks onboard the ship with him. — I joined the ship in the Antarctic, Norway and the Arctic Circle, Costa Rica, and Florida And when he was home, we took off on road trips throughout Canada and the US. Years of adventure I would have missed out on if I hadn't listened to my intuition and taken that leap of faith to fly to Ireland and meet a man.

Although the relationship ended and we didn't get married (remember the Maui trip in chapter 6?!), it was still worthwhile. Love is always worth the risk of getting hurt.

Arriving in London, UK

Guernsey, Channel Islands

Saint-Malo, France

The High Price of Ignoring Intuition

Intuition can also whisper and sometimes be hard to hear, if we're not listening.

My first car was a 1984 Camaro, red with a T-roof. I had spotted it one day with a for sale sign in the window as I passed by on the school bus. Every day, the bus went by and I stared longingly out the window. This was the coolest car I had ever seen, and it was my favourite color — I had to have it.

Much to my mom's surprise, Dad said, "Yes!" He took me to test drive the car, gave it a mechanical inspection, and helped me get set up with a loan at the bank. Soon I was cruising around town with the roof off and Bryan Adams blasting from the cassette player. I was 17 years old and thought I was pretty cool.

Dad had recently retired from the Royal Canadian Mounted Police (RCMP) and my parents decided to move to Alberta for cattle ranching, but I was still in grade 12 and decided to stay in Penticton. My older brother was dating a girl in Vancouver, so he stayed as well and we got our first place together — a two-bedroom, one bathroom fully furnished condo. We were two kids who had no idea what we were doing but tried our best! I'll always remember the first time we made perogies — they were burnt black on the outside and still frozen inside!

Here I was, 17 years old, still in high school, living on my own, cruising in my cool car and working part-time after school to pay for everything. I loved this car. I washed it all the time and took great care of it, but I was still a kid.

I came home late one night, after hanging out with friends. I parked the car and stood there for a moment contemplating. The T-roof panels were off and tucked away in the back. I knew I should take a minute to put them back on and secure the vehicle, but I was tired. I remember a little voice saying, "It will only take a few minutes," and I responded with, "Nah, I'm tired. It will be fine."

A part of me knew it wouldn't be fine – I'd later come to learn this was my intuition, and a voice I could ignore at my own peril.

I went to bed and didn't give it a second thought. I came out in the morning ready to head to school and stopped as I saw the passenger side window smashed. I ran over and looked inside. One of the T-roof panels was gone.

I was so ashamed. I knew I was supposed to put them back properly the night before, and I didn't. I was embarrassed to file a police report because I felt it was my fault. But I filed the police report and paid my insurance deductible and had to drive around with plastic covering the roof and window for a few days while waiting for the replacement parts to arrive.

I grew up through that process and learned a lesson that has stayed with me: When you have a "feeling," when you hear a voice say, "No," when your body has a strong reaction, you listen. You don't question it, you don't try to figure it out – you simply listen. And life will flow much smoother for you.

Knowing yourself and knowing what's right for you is key to helping you navigate life and be happy.

The Courage to Be Yourself

I grew up in a big family. I have three brothers and one sister, and it was always chaotic but fun. My mom said all she ever wanted to be was a mom and it showed. She had endless energy to keep up with us, she constantly created new adventures, she included us in her daily routine and somehow made chores into a game. She appeared to thrive being a mom and I marveled at her self-assurance.

I never felt that longing to be a mom. And I felt I had to keep that to myself, like a dark secret. As a woman, society expected me to have children. It seemed like the traditional path of getting married and having children is what you did. And I didn't personally know anyone who chose a different path.

But it didn't feel right for me. When I checked in with my intuition and asked if children were right for me, I always got a strong "No."

For years, I felt like I was carrying around this dirty secret: I didn't want to have kids. It wasn't something people talked about, it was just assumed, so I kept quiet — until one day I couldn't do it anymore.

I was 21 years old and working as a legal secretary in a large law firm. One of the partners was hosting a Christmas party and invited all the staff to attend. My boyfriend and I got dressed up and went to the party. And as often happens at parties, a group of us ended up in the kitchen.

People were talking about holiday plans, and recipes, and their children. Someone turned to me and said, "So Michelle, when are you guys having kids?" Without thinking, I blurted out, "Oh, no, I'm not having kids."

Every conversation in the kitchen stopped.

It felt like everybody turned to look at me in shock. "What do you mean you're not going to have kids?"

I froze. Why had I shared that out loud?

Here I was at a fancy party with all the law firm partners and their wives, people with traditional views, and I was rocking the boat.

I took a deep breath and said, "Kids aren't for me." I naively thought that was the end of the conversation. I had thought about it, made a decision that was best for me, and was living my life.

But the women in that room were not happy. Suddenly they all had an opinion. "You're young. You'll change your mind." Nope, I don't think so.

"Maybe you just haven't found the right person." Well, I'm here with my boyfriend of three years and it's going pretty great. I still don't want kids.

"But who will take care of you when you're old?" Umm, I don't think that's a great reason to have kids.

Finally, they wore me down and I thought it was easier to just agree that I might one day change my mind so we could move on to a different topic.

But the experience rattled me. Women can choose different paths, right? Was I wrong to want something different for my life?

The next day, my colleague Daphne came to see me. She had been in the kitchen and witnessed the conversation and my discomfort. She said, "You know, Michelle, that's great that you've decided not to have children, but you can't say it out loud. It's upsetting to some people."

It was hard for me to hear because I thought people should be able to make their own decisions and we'd support them, but it was a cold dose of reality. Daphne had chosen not to have children and was happy with her decision but learned to be quiet when those conversations arose. I was glad she reached out to me but also sad that I was expected to keep quiet about not wanting children. I felt lonely and alone.

Even though I knew people thought I'd change my mind, I had tuned into my intuition, I was self-aware, and I knew what was right for me. I realized that didn't mean other people were going to be happy for me, or support me and that's where resilience comes in.

Because you want people to support what makes you happy. And some people aren't going to support you. It could be people that you love. It could be your parents. It could be a partner, it could be anybody. And so how do you bounce back from that when your usual fan club and your usual support team isn't on board?

It's hard. That's when you pull out all your resilience tools — you look at self-awareness and remember what brings you joy. The bottom line is you need to be true to yourself. Because if you make a decision to make other people happy, when you know it's not what you need, you're not going to be happy.

Fear vs. Intuition: How to Tell the Difference

Sometimes intuition requires a leap of faith, and sometimes our mind can play tricks on us. So listen to your heart and get your mind out of it!

When I was in New Zealand with Kris (my youngest brother) and Jana (my sister), Kris and I decided to go skydiving. It was something we'd always wanted to do so why not do it in New Zealand? We found a place in Taupo and signed up. We were scheduled for 10:30am the next day and crossed our fingers for good weather, as the previous day's jumps had been cancelled due to wind.

We arrived the next morning feeling excited and nervous. We put on jumpsuits and the staff helped us into harnesses. We were jumping tandem, attached to an instructor because we'd never jumped before. There was a short briefing of what to do, what not do, and then they were leading us across a field to the smallest plane I'd ever seen. There was only one seat — for the pilot — and the rest of us sat on the floor with our knees up to our ears.

As usual, I'm all about grand ideas and charge in with, "Let's do this thing. That sounds amazing!" and then reality hits me and I doubt all my decisions.

The plane took off and was circling higher and higher. I looked down and said, "Oh, this doesn't look so bad." And the pilot responded, "Yeah, we're about halfway up there." Gulp.

When we reached 12,000 feet, things happened fast. They threw open the door and before I could say, "Good luck," Kris was gone.

My heart stopped.

Everything around me froze and I couldn't hear anything.

My brother had just fallen out of a plane.

My mind knew we were jumping out of a plane, and everything was going to be fine. I knew this was the plan. Kris was hooked up with the instructor, they would pull the parachute, and everything was good. My brain understood but there seemed to be a time delay.

My eyes had seen my little brother falling out of a plane. I gasped as I reached for him, but I was too late.

I don't know how to describe that fear, losing someone you love before your eyes. There was a severe disconnect between my heart and head and I couldn't process what had just happened.

I think I went into shock. The next thing I knew, they had pushed me out (strapped to my instructor) and we were in freefall.

I was still terrified about what had happened to my brother, and it felt like I was in a dream. We were moving so fast, and the air was so cold, I felt like I couldn't breathe. I didn't make a sound.

We fell for 7,000 feet, which was the longest, scariest 45 seconds of my life! When the instructor finally pulled the chute, we jerked to a stop and my body relaxed. It was beautiful. I could see for miles and miles in every direction — the mountains, the lake, the city. It was so peaceful. I could have stayed up there forever.

We slowly made our approach and gently glided down. It was surprisingly soft and easy to land. As soon as I was detached from the harness, I ran full speed to Kris and gave him the biggest hug ever. He was alive! I hadn't lost him after all! My heart and head and eyes had finally synched.

Jana joined us and we all laughed and hugged and held onto each other until our legs stopped shaking. I was so proud of us for doing it and thrilled to share the experience with my siblings.

To this day, when a strong gust of wind catches my breath, it takes me right back to freefalling from a plane in New Zealand and that mix of fear and intuition.

We've talked about intuition and its role with resilience, but sometimes we can confuse fear and intuition. Fear is a good thing — it keeps us safe, so we need to listen to our fear and honor it. But sometimes it takes courage and conviction to do just that.

Pre-jump excitement (with instructor)

Still smiling...in the plane, Lake Taupo, New Zealand

We survived! Kris and I embrace after skydiving

Learning to Listen: A Lesson from the River

On month four of my Remote Year, we were living in Sofia, Bulgaria. Bulgaria is beautiful and surrounded by nature, and Bulgarians are active, outdoorsy people who love to hike up mountains, raft down rivers and recharge in hot springs.

The city team had organized a day of whitewater rafting and many of my friends excitedly signed up. I had zero interest, as I've had friends who drowned, so the idea of getting into an inflatable raft and purposely bouncing off rocks in rushing water didn't sound smart.

Since we were now a third of the way through our 12-month journey, many people were reviewing their finances more closely, including myself. I was chatting with a friend about all the activities we could do and mentioned that I wasn't doing some of them due to costs.

My friend Lindsay overheard part of the conversation and thought I wanted to go whitewater rafting but couldn't afford it, so she bought me a ticket to go!

She was so excited to surprise me, and I was so overwhelmed by her generosity. We stood there crying and laughing and hugging, and I didn't have the heart to tell her I didn't want to go. I thought maybe this was a sign that I should go and get over my fear.

I tried to smile but noticed my heart rate had increased.

Over the next two days, I couldn't sleep. I tossed and turned and woke up drenched in sweat, panicked from dreams I couldn't recall. I prayed for bad weather so the event would be cancelled.

When the list came out to confirm who was going, my name wasn't on it and I secretly rejoiced — did they overbook and there wasn't room for me?! But no, they had listed another Michelle by mistake, and I was confirmed. Crap!

The morning came for us to go, and I was a wreck. I considered backing out but put on what I hoped was a brave face and met the group for the two-hour drive.

The bus was silent as everyone fell asleep but that wasn't an option for me. I stared out the window at the beautiful scenery and tried to control my breathing.

When we arrived, I tracked down our guide and explained my fears. She assured me everything would be fine. I suited up and we headed down to the river for the safety demonstration.

I'm sure they have to cover every possible scenario that will likely never happen, but as the list of possibilities went on and she continued to say, "If this happens, don't panic," I could feel myself already panicking and tears started to escape from my eyes.

But the clincher came when she asked the group to separate into two rafts: one for those who were a little nervous or beginners and one for those experienced or who wanted more thrills.

Everyone stepped away from me and I stood at the beginner raft all alone.

No one wanted to come with me.

At that moment, I never felt so lonely — so homesick for my friends who would have stood by me and put their arms around me for support.

It felt like hours that I stood there alone until I heard someone say, "I'll come with you, Michelle."

I looked up and saw Justin, one of the youngest, most athletic guys walking towards me, someone I knew wanted to be in the "thrill" raft. He gave me a hug; told me everything would be okay and the floodgate of tears opened.

Slowly our raft filled with others, and we were off. My body was visibly shaking but I pressed on.

"Forward!" "Back!" "Forward!" "Stop!" Our guide continued to yell instructions as we went along. Our first rapids approached, and I held my breath. We made it without issue, but I felt nauseous. The guide asked if I was okay and I said, "No, this is not fun." She simply smiled and said, "It's okay."

The second rapids came up and I was terrified. We hit a boulder, knocking one of the girls into the bottom of the raft, and then started going backwards as a huge wave crashed over the raft and I was paralyzed with fear.

Our guide moved us to the side of the river and looked at me. "Do you want to get off?"

"Hell, yes!"

I scrambled out of the raft, knees shaking as I climbed the bank and joined the photographer.

The rest of the group carried on down the river and I rode in the van with the photographer, trying to calm my racing heart.

When we met again at the end of the river, I was relieved to see everyone safe and sound. I enjoyed hearing their adventures and never once doubted my decision to get out of the raft early.

It wasn't a fear I needed to "get over" — it was my intuition telling me it wasn't right for me. Your body knows the truth, you just have to be willing to listen.

Now, if I had told my friend from the beginning that I didn't want to go, I would have saved myself days of anxiety. I'm sure she would have understood but I didn't want to appear ungrateful.

Lesson learned: You will never disappoint someone if you speak the truth. It is far more damaging to keep it buried inside.

And if every cell in your body is screaming, "Don't do this!" listen to that inner voice and make a choice that feels better.

Me, terrified, in the red life jacket, Bulgaria

The next time you're feeling overwhelmed and don't know whether it's fear or intuition, try these steps to find out what's really going on.

1. **Sit down and breathe.** When our hearts are racing, we can feel tense in our body, and it's hard to hear what our body is trying to say. Taking a moment to focus on our breathing helps relax the body and let it know it's safe.

2. **Identify the issue and break it down.** If we can get clear about the issue in front of us and focus on the core problem, our brain can then focus

on solutions. Break it down to one question, if possible, such as: "Do I want to change careers?" "Should I move to a smaller town?" or "Do I want to go whitewater rafting?"

3. **Notice where you're feeling sensations.** Ask the question then sit quietly for a few minutes and see what comes up. Is there a tightness in your chest? Are your palms sweaty? Is there negative self-talk running through your head? Try to name the feelings (e.g., worry, nervousness, anticipation, peace, shame, etc.). See what comes up and continue to listen to your body. You can also ask questions like, "What are you telling me?" and see what answers arise.

4. **Be patient.** When feelings of fear surface, we tend to either avoid or repress them, or over analyze. Give yourself time (a few days or even weeks) to allow the answer to "come to you."

The Get Bendy lesson here is to trust your intuition, the answers are always inside of you. You just need to believe, have patience and slow down to listen for your truth.

Get Bendy Reflection Questions

Ask yourself:

- When have I relied on my intuition in the past, and what was the outcome?
- How do I distinguish between intuition and rational thinking in decision- making?
- In what areas of my life do I trust my intuition the most, and why?
- Am I living true to myself?
- Where am I on my journey?

Get Bendy Exercise

Take a different route to work. When you come to an intersection, ask yourself, "Left or right?" and pause. See if you can feel what your body is telling you.

Or

Sit quietly and take a few deep breaths. Think of a decision, like whether to accept a job offer. Notice any immediate gut feelings or physical sensations — do you feel excited or uneasy? Reflect on how these feelings align with your logical thoughts. Trust your intuition and consider how it guides your decision.

CONCLUSION

esilience is the ability to bounce back from whatever life throws at you. Some people are better at this than others, but the good news is, anyone can learn and get better at it.

If you look back at your childhood, can you remember times when things didn't work out as planned? For me, I remember being about nine years old, living on a farm in Dawson Creek, B.C. and being in 4-H, an agricultural youth development program.

In 4-H, we pledge:
> My HEAD to clearer thinking,
> My HEART to greater loyalty,
> My HANDS to larger service,
> My HEALTH to better living,

For my Club, my Community, my Country and my World.

I was in the beef livestock program, where you were responsible for raising a steer (young neutered male cattle). Training included caring for the young calf, feeding, keeping records, and fitting and showmanship techniques. At the end of the program, the steer is sold at auction.

Somehow, I didn't remember hearing the part about selling them at the end, so I poured my heart into loving my steer (who I named "Danny," after the boy I had a crush on at school). I got up early each morning to go feed Danny, talk to him and scratch behind his ears. I ran to see him at the barn as soon as I got home from school to tell him about my day while I brushed his fluffy brown hair. I dutifully recorded notes about how much I fed him, his current weight and anything else I noticed.

Danny and I were best friends, and I didn't need a halter to lead him around — he followed me.

When the big "show" day finally came, I was excited to give Danny a bath and make him look his best. I put on my new jeans and my red 4-H vest, Mom French-braided my hair, and I proudly led Danny into the ring.

It was full of people and noise, and I was overwhelmed. The auctioneer was speaking a mile a minute and suddenly yelled, "Sold!"

A man started walking toward me to take away Danny and I flung my arms around Danny's neck and started crying. I cried and cried and hung on as tightly as my little arms could.

What happened next is a blur. Perhaps I've blocked it from my memory because it was too hard, but I remember feeling devastated, heartbroken and confused.

My parents didn't try to distract me, they didn't tell me everything would be okay, they didn't ignore me — they just let me cry, let me be sad, let me grieve this loss, something I didn't see coming.

I can still feel that little girl's heartache and it taught me a valuable lesson — life is going to surprise you and it's okay to feel whatever emotion hits you. The important thing is to allow yourself to feel those emotions and then figure out how you move forward.

Life has thrown me many surprises, some good, some not so good, but over time, I've developed skills to help me get back up quicker each time.

I've learned the importance of creating an environment to support my needs, and how to get what I want while working with what I have.

I Found My Way Home

My soul longs to be near water and I'm happiest when I have lots of natural light. My home in Penticton, B.C. was comfortable, it had all the space I needed, it was affordable and looked out over a beautiful Northern Pine Oak tree. But I couldn't see the lake and it only had one large window. I felt a longing for something more and began to search for properties with lake views and natural light.

More than 1.5 years later, I still hadn't found what I was looking for and felt frustrated. Then I realized I was trying to control the "how" instead of focusing on the end result. I thought I had to sell my current home and buy something new but that was just one option. There were many ways my dream could come true, I just needed to hold onto the vision and manifest it.

Once I got out of my own way, things happened in less than one week. I realized I could rent out my current home and go rent the home I really wanted.

I opened Facebook Marketplace, and there was the exact house I was dreaming of — tall ceilings, floor-to-ceiling windows and sweeping views of the lake. I wrote to the owner, knowing the place was mine. We met the next day and signed the paperwork.

Then I posted an advertisement to rent out my home, met with a great guy the following evening and he signed paperwork for my place.

Seemingly "just like that," I had manifested my soul's desire — lots of natural light and water views. But I've had years of practice of getting clear about what I want, aligning my thoughts and actions, and believing with unshakable confidence that it will happen.

Getting bendy is a skill that can be learned and developed with practice. Remember to stay positive and surround yourself with like-minded people who are going to cheer you on and support you. And as you go through life's ups and downs, be self-aware and find things that bring you joy.

Take care of yourself. Listen to your intuition. Accept where you are, even when things are hard, and allow yourself to know that you have everything you need to be able to move through it with grace and love.

I used to feel guilty that I should be so happy, and then I found a beautiful quote (and I do not know who said it!):

"Do not be ashamed of what makes you happy. Whatever it is. And do not give up on what fills you with joy. No matter how much time it takes."

That is my wish for you — that you find the things that bring you joy, that you get up when life knocks you down and that you find a way to live a life that you love.

Grand Canyon, Arizona

Istanbul, Turkey

Lunenberg, Nova Scotia, Canada

Fresh seafood on Prince Edward Island, Canada

CONCLUSION

New Zealand

Lord of the Rings Hobbiton movie set, New Zealand

Oregon Coast, USA

Finding my wings in Turkey

CONCLUSION

Montevideo, Uruguay

ABOUT THE AUTHOR

Michelle Hargrave is a force of resilience, adventure, and laughter. By day, she navigates the corridors of power as an executive for the British Columbia government. But by passion, she's a globetrotter, a laughter yoga practitioner, and a relentless seeker of growth.

With more than 35 countries stamped in her passport, Michelle believes that travel isn't just about exploring new landscapes — it's about expanding the horizons of the mind and heart. As a certified laughter yoga practitioner, she knows the transformative power of finding joy even in the face of adversity.

Driven by a deep conviction that travel is the ultimate bridge to understanding, Michelle invites readers to dust off their passports and embark on their own journeys of discovery. Through her infectious enthusiasm and unyielding spirit, she inspires others to embrace life's uncertainties and find resilience in every adventure.

So, join Michelle on this exhilarating journey. Let her stories ignite your wanderlust and empower you to live a life filled with laughter, exploration, and boundless growth. The world is waiting — are you ready to answer the call?

www.michellehargrave.com

Made in United States
Troutdale, OR
12/04/2024